WILLIAM STYRON

Say what you will, to be a critic is very decent, but not nearly so hard as to be a writer.

—WS

WILLIAM STYRON

AN ANNOTATED BIBLIOGRAPHY OF CRITICISM

Compiled by
PHILIP W. LEON

GREENWOOD PRESS

Westport, Connecticut • London, England

Library of Congress Cataloging in Publication Data

Leon, Philip W
    William Styron, an annotated bibliography of criticism.

    Includes indexes.
      1. Styron, William, 1925-   --Bibliography.
I. Title.
Z8852.4.L46   [PS3569.T9]   016.813'5'4   78-60256
ISBN 0-313-20558-2   813 Styron

Library of Congress Catalog Card Number: 78-60256
ISBN: 0-313-20558-2

First published in 1978

Greenwood Press, Inc.
51 Riverside Avenue, Westport, Connecticut 06880

Printed in the United States of America

10 9 8 7 6 5 4 3 2 1

For Joan

CONTENTS

PREFACE

The purpose of this compilation is to provide scholars and teachers with a comprehensive list of secondary sources to aid them in a study of the works of William Styron, a writer to be read. The Phi Beta Kappa graduate of Duke University has been called "too highbrow" by one critic and "too lowbrow" by another. One critic praises him; another disparages him. The annotated entries reveal this diversity of critical opinion.

Styron has long been a popular figure in college literature courses as evidenced by the numerous Ph.D. dissertations written about him. These dissertations are annotated for the first time. Also annotated are previous bibliographies, books containing chapters on or references to Styron, and critical articles from scholarly journals.

Annotations consist of brief summaries or, when appropriate, representative excerpts from the criticism itself. Book reviews are categorized according to primary work. Because Styron figures prominently in non-literary activities, a special section of references to Styron in *The New York Times* is included to add a dimension to the man behind the writing.

Several people helped me with this study. Initial funding for this book came from the Citadel Development Foundation. Styron, through his friendship, courtesy, and correspondence, has made my research a keen professional pleasure. The influence of Dr. Warren I. Titus of Peabody College has been profound. Melvin Friedman of the University of Wisconsin-Milwaukee, and James L. W. West III of Virginia Polytechnic Institute and State University, early and recent Styron scholars, were generous in making available special material. The staffs of the Duke University Library and the Library of Congress were most helpful with manuscripts. The Wake Forest University Library, with its excellent resources, proved to be a treasure-trove of material.

Mary Furlow provided valuable assistance with correspondence; Frances Rosier typed the manuscript and, incredibly, remained my friend all the while. I appreciate the encouragement given me by my wife, by Dr. A.H. Blair, and by my colleagues in the English department at The Citadel.

Philip W. Leon

The Citadel
January 1978

WILLIAM STYRON

INTRODUCTION

William Styron: His Life and Career

Richard D. Altick, speaking of authors generally, says that "behind the book is a man or woman whose character and experience of life cannot be overlooked in any effort to establish what the book really says." The books and articles contained in this study show the range of critical attention that Styron's works have received throughout his career. Perhaps a brief look at Styron's life will assist the critics for whom this book is intended by revealing the patterns and textures of the man behind the writings.

Styron was born in Newport News, Virginia, on June 11, 1925. His father, William Clark Styron, was an engineer at the Newport News shipyard. His mother, Pauline Margaret Abraham Styron, died when Styron was thirteen. An energetic youth, he was sent to Christchurch, a well-disciplined Episcopal preparatory school in Virginia. In May 1975, he was to return to deliver the commencement address.

At Davidson College, a scholastically demanding Presbyterian college near Charlotte, North Carolina, he studied with other young southern gentlemen, receiving what is now regarded as a traditional education grounded in the classics, overlaid with a proper Protestant sense of hard work and discipline. World War II was imminent, and Styron enlisted as did many others at all-male Davidson. The Marine Corps sent Styron to Duke University in the V-12 program. (Many men of talent were so favored until the program ended.) Styron served honorably in the Pacific Theater toward the end of the war. In the war zone he was spared the heaviest and grimmest part of the fighting. He is proud of his participation in the war, though his attitude toward the military changed after his first-hand experience. His participation in World War II and as a reservist recalled during the Korean War lay at the core of several of his published and unpublished works. The best-known of these, *The Long March*, renders in excruciatingly realistic detail the agony of marines on a forced road march. A lesser-known work, Styron's play, *In the Clap Shack*, uses humor instead of suffering to reveal Styron's deep mistrust and dislike of the military.

Styron spent 1946 in Italy helping with the recovery from the war. The next year he returned to Duke, graduated, and went to New York City. The only regular job Styron ever held was a short, unhappy stint as a copy editor and book jacket blurb writer for McGraw-Hill Book Company. There Styron resolved to give himself full-time to the writing he knew he was capable of producing. In a mad moment Styron showed up at the staid publishing firm wearing his old Marine cap and a seersucker suit. His audacity in sailing paper airplanes and in floating soap bubbles from the windows of the McGraw-Hill building sealed the end of his career—at least at that end of the publishing industry.

Financed by his father, Styron enrolled in the New School for Social Research. There he conceived and began *Lie Down in Darkness*, a novel about a girl from Virginia who commits suicide in New York City by leaping from the top floor of a tenement building. Many critics regard Styron's first novel as his best. Certainly for a writer so young Styron showed unusual maturity and craftsmanship in his fiction.

Styron's slow pace of composition, writing and rewriting only two to three pages a day, was quickened by his recall to active duty with the Marine Corps to serve in Korea. He barely handed over his manuscript of *Lie Down in Darkness* when he reported to Camp Lejeune, North Carolina. He never went to Korea, obtaining a release from service because of an eye ailment. Almost as though he wanted to dissociate himself from the government that attempted to return him to the fighting, Styron left for Europe.

In France with Peter Matthiessen and George Plimpton, he founded *The Paris Review*. When so many of the little magazines failed, this one flourished and remains a prestigious outlet for creative fiction and poetry. Styron and his literary set had no illusions about their relationship to another band of expatriates—Hemingway, Fitzgerald, Dos Passos, and the like. Styron's generation of writers followed the group Gertrude Stein labeled the Lost Generation. In *Lie Down in Darkness*, Peyton Loftis says her father's generation was not lost. Rather they were losing the next, i.e., Styron's generation.

Styron is enormously popular in France. *Lie Down in Darkness* was named to the *Agregation*, the reading list for French universities, for 1973-1974. Styron was the only living author on the list; Hawthorne and Poe were the only other Americans named that year. His writings are amenable to the French *nouveau roman* genre, particularly *Set This House on Fire*, the work perhaps the least well-received in the United States of all of Styron's novels. Styron's experiences in Italy, the principal setting of the book, and in France, inform this ambitious and bulky novel about an American artist who tries to "find himself" in Europe.

Expatriates usually come home, and so did Styron in 1953. He met Rose Burgunder at Johns Hopkins, and a short time later that year, in Rome, they were married. Rose Styron is a published writer, having collaborated on a volume of Russian poems in translation and having had published a collection of her own poems. She is Styron's best critic of his works in progress and helps maintain his ties to *The Paris Review* as a contributing poetry editor. The Styrons have four children, Susanna, Paola, Thomas, and Alexandra. He and his family live in Roxbury, Connecticut, and spend their summers at their home on Martha's Vineyard.

While Styron has mused that he may someday return to his native south, he is firmly settled in the north, his ties to Yale University being particularly strong. He was named as a Fellow of Silliman College at Yale in 1964. In 1972, the Yale Repertory Theatre staged his play, *In the Clap Shack*, the second major work growing out of his Marine Corps experiences.

A winner of numerous prizes and awards, Styron has a firm place among modern American writers. *Lie Down in Darkness* was a candidate for the Pulitzer Prize and won the Prix de Rome of the American Academy of Arts and Letters. In 1963 he was named to the Board of Directors of the Inter-American Foundation of the Arts, and in 1970 to the editorial board of *The American Scholar*. That same year he was the recipient of the Howells Medal of the National Association of Arts and Letters.

The most distinguished of his honors is the Pulitzer Prize for his 1967 novel, *The Confessions of Nat Turner*, the work that brought Styron at once hostile fire and great admiration from the academic community. He has honorary doctorates from Wilberforce University, Duke University, the New School for Social Research, and Tufts University. In 1976 he received the University Union Award for Distinction in Literature at the University of South Carolina, an award previously given to Robert Penn Warren, Robert Lowell, and Archibald Macleish.

II

Having achieved these personal and professional measures of success, it would doubtless be exceedingly easy for Styron to remain cloistered in Roxbury, an idyllic woodland setting, content to play tennis with his neighbor Arthur Miller. Certainly the royalties from works already published would allow him to live handsomely. But his inability to hide from difficulty makes Styron the novelist he is; without his driving need to confront the ills and hellishness of life, Styron would not have written with the knowledge of psychology that is *Lie Down in Darkness*, the brutality that is *The Long March*, the chaos that is *Set This House on Fire*, and the rebellion that is *The Confessions of Nat Turner*. Styron is not a complacent man; neither are his novels complacent works.

His slow, ritualistic pace of writing could symbolize his view that modern man will succeed by persistence. Styron knows this, and his major characters, explosive and sometimes aberrant, come to know it. Peyton Loftis of *Lie Down in Darkness* finds out too late and plummets to her death; Captain Mannix, the rebellious hero of *The Long March*, limping and nearly defeated, is figuratively clubbed over the head with that truth; Cass Kinsolving of *Set This House on Fire* arrives at an existential formula for surviving one day at a time; and Nat Turner, the rebellious slave, burns himself out at an early age before he realizes that sudden change enacted through violence is foredoomed.

The William Styron of today only partly resembles the William Styron whose novels carry such an impact and shock effect that critics are still looking for the common denominator by which to assess him. Styron is still a rebel who shakes his fist at conformity, but he has grown increasingly more mature as a writer. Styron's novels show characters who are not afraid of battles, just as Styron himself does not avoid social battles for causes he believes in.

Styron's books are as popular in the Soviet Union as they are in France. He once said in an interview that he feels 'at home" in both places because of the friendly receptions given his work. But his true feelings emerged later when he stirred up a minor tempest in 1969 commenting on the defection of Anatoly Kuznetsov from the Soviet Union, saying that the Soviet author's action could endanger other dissidents in the U.S.S.R.

Styron had to clarify his statement lest he be interpreted as advocating docile acceptance of their lot by Soviet writers, artists,ʹ and intellectuals. He said he deplored Kuznetsov's "precipitate haste" in denouncing the Soviet Union in such a way as to endanger other writers. Styron also said he found, on a three-week trip to Moscow, the oppression so unbearable that he "became desperate to get out again."

He became involved in the cause of Soviet writers again in 1972, when he joined such writers as Saul Bellow, Herbert Mitgang, Malcolm Cowley, Bernard Malamud, Louis Auchincloss, Norman Mailer, Lionel Trilling, and Rex Stout in sending a letter to Soviet President Podgorny urging him to restore fundamental human rights to Soviet Jews. The writers particularly wanted to see restored cultural and educational opportunities which were being denied. While Styron is neither a Soviet nor a Jew, he does not hesitate to enter struggles of this sort. As his fiction and his public utterances give testimony, any struggle for human rights is Styron's struggle.

One of those public utterances came in court when Styron testified that he saw Chicago police beat demonstrators in Lincoln Park during the 1968 Democratic Convention. As a pro-McCarthy alternate delegate to the convention, Styron was present in Chicago to witness at first-hand the brutality inflicted on young people demonstrating against the Vietnam War. Styron subsequently put politics back into the hands of the professional politicians, largely because of the "dirtiness" he observed in 1968.

Styron and neighbor Arthur Miller often find themselves on the same side of social issues. When a teacher in their hometown of Roxbury, Connecticut, was suspended for refusing to say the Pledge of Allegiance with her classes, Styron and Miller, along with two dozen local residents, signed a statement protesting the suspension. Styron is not anti-American; rather, Styron is pro-Americans and their civil liberties.

Styron once became involved in prison reform through the case of Benjamin Reid, a black man who faced certain death in the electric chair until Styron led a crusade to have his sentence commuted to life imprisonment. Sadly, Styron had to dissociate himself from Reid's cause when Reid escaped from a work crew and went on a rampage of violence shortly before he was due for parole. There can be little doubt that the irony was not lost on Styron that Reid, like Styron's Nat Turner, rebelled violently in the face of kindness. Though Styron could hardly condone Reid's behavior, he could appreciate the forces that drove him to his abortive attempt to be free: a prison—or slave—system cannot be benevolent. Much of the hostile criticism from black intellectuals toward *The Confessions of*

Nat Turner springs from Styron's attempt at a psychological portrait showing Turner as a proud black man who comes to resent the favors shown him by his white masters. The dust appears to have settled on the controversial novel, and critics generally regard the book as a masterful work of contemporary fiction.

Styron's experience with prison reform was not soured by his disappointment with Benjamin Reid. In 1975 Styron joined Miller and Director Mike Nichols in establishing a defense fund for an eighteen-year-old boy convicted in 1973 for the manslaughter of his mother in Canaan, Connecticut, near Styron's home. Miller noticed some discrepancies in the case, concluding that the boy was psychologically incapable of committing the crime. Styron and Nichols joined the cause. They hired a new lawyer and secured coverage of the story in *The New York Times*. Because of their influence, the investigation was re-opened, another suspect arrested, and the boy cleared. But for the concern of Styron and others in the community, the young man would be languishing in prison. Joan Barthel's *A Death in Canaan* (1976) details the case; Styron wrote the introduction to Barthel's book.

Recently Styron became involved in examining the motivations behind the Nazi concentration camps in which millions of Jews were slaughtered. His interest stems in part from research for a forthcoming novel about a woman who survives such a camp. Following a tour of Auschwitz, Styron called the holocaust "awesomely central to our present-day consciousness." For Styron, the Nazi totalitarianism that produced the barbarity of Auschwitz is a living message to the present, not a ghastly chapter in a history book that gathers dust on the shelf.

The non-literary portrait of Styron, revealed by his public stand on controversial issues, reflects the degree of intense concern that Styron gives to his fictional characters. Behind Styron's books is a man whose experience of life informs his writing. For critics who deal with literary works in order to discover "what the book really says," and for scholars who enjoy seeing both the development of a writer and his effects upon the world of which he writes, this book is proffered.

CHRONOLOGY

1925   William Styron is born June 11, in Newport News, Virginia.

1938   Styron's mother dies. This same year Styron enters Christchurch Preparatory School in Virginia.

1942   Styron enters Davidson College near Charlotte, North Carolina.

1943   As a Marine Styron enters Duke University in Durham, North Carolina, as a member of the V-12 Program. At Duke he publishes his first short stories in the student literary magazine, *The Archive*.

1946   Styron goes to Italy to help in recovery from the war.

1947   Styron receives his bachelor's degree from Duke and takes a job at McGraw-Hill reading manuscripts and writing book jacket blurbs. Later that year he enrolls in the New School for Social Research.

1948   Under the guidance of Hiram Hadyn at the New School, Styron begins work on his first novel, *Lie Down in Darkness*.

1950   Recalled to active duty with the Marines for the Korean War, Styron barely has time to finish *Lie Down in Darkness*.

1951   Styron is discharged from the Marines; *Lie Down in Darkness* is published.

1952   Styron leaves for Paris; his first novel wins the Prix de Rome of the American Academy. In Paris he becomes one of the founders of *Paris Review* along with George Plimpton and Peter Matthiessen. Styron continues to serve as an Advisory Editor to *Paris Review*.

1953   He returns to America and is introduced to Rose Burgunder by Louis Rubin at Johns Hopkins. Later that year in Rome they marry. *The Long March* is published in *Discovery*, No. 1.

1954   The Styrons settle in Roxbury, Connecticut, and he begins *Set This House on Fire*, incorporating his recent European travels and experiences into the novel.

1960   *Set This House on Fire* is published by Random House, and Styron begins work on *The Confessions of Nat Turner* about the Southampton County, Virginia, slave insurrection of 1831.

1963   Styron is named as a member of the Board of Directors of the Inter-American Foundation of Arts.

1964   Styron is named a Fellow of Silliman College, Yale.

1967   *The Confessions of Nat Turner* is published by Random House.

1968   Styron receives the Pulitzer Prize for *The Confessions of Nat Turner*. He receives honorary degrees from Wilberforce University, Ohio; Duke University, Durham, North Carolina; The New School for Social Research, New York; and Tufts University, Medford, Massachusetts.

1970   Styron works on *The Way of the Warrior*, another novel about the Marines. Styron has put this book away uncompleted. He is named a member of the Editorial Board of *The American Scholar*.

1973 Styron is named to the Duke University chapter of Phi Beta
Kappa. He begins work on *Sophie's Choice,* a novel about a
woman who survives a Nazi concentration camp.

1976 Styron receives the University Union Award for distinction
in Literature from the University of South Carolina.

PRIMARY
SOURCES

NOVELS

1. *Lie Down in Darkness*
   Indianapolis and New York: Bobbs-Merrill, 1951.
   London: Hamish Hamilton, 1952.
   New York: New American Library/Signet, 1952.
   London: Transworld Publishers/Corgi, 1961.
   Indianapolis and New York: Bobbs-Merrill/Literary Guild, 1968.

2. *The Long March*
   New York: Modern Library Paperback, 1956.
   London: Hamish Hamilton, 1962.
   Harmondsworth, Middlesex: Penguin, 1964.
   New York: New American Library/Signet, 1968.
   New York: New American Library/Plume, 1975. Double volume with *In the Clap Shack*.

3. *Set This House on Fire*
   New York: Random House, 1960.
   New York: New American Library/Signet, 1961.
   London: Transworld Publishers/Corgi, 1963.

4. *The Confessions of Nat Turner*
   New York: Random House, 1967.
   New York: New American Library/Signet, 1968.
   London: Panther, 1968.

SHORT STORIES

1. "Autumn." *One and Twenty: Duke Narrative and Verse, 1924-1945.* Ed. William Blackburn. Durham, North Carolina: Duke University Press, 1945.

2. "The Brothers." Typescript of an unpublished short story. Duke University Library Archives. (*The Archive* is the student literary magazine at Styron's alma mater, Duke University.)

3. "The Enormous Window." *American Vanguard, 1950.* Ed. Charles I. Glicksberg. New York: New School for Social Research, 1950.

4. "The Force of Her Happiness." *The Archive,* 89 (Spring 1977), 94-114.

5. "The Long Dark Road." *One and Twenty: Duke Narrative and Verse, 1924-1945.* Ed.William Blackburn. Durham, North Carolina: Duke University Press, 1945.

6. "The McCabes." *Paris Review,* 6 (Autumn-Winter 1960), 12-28. (This short story was later incorporated into Chapter VI of *Set This House on Fire.)*

7. "Marriott, the Marine." *Esquire,* September 1971, pp. 100-4, 196, 198, 200, 202, 204, 207, 208, 210. (Chapter I of *The Way of the Warrior,* a novel which Styron has had on and off the shelf several times.)

8. "A Moment in Trieste." *American Vanguard, 1948.* Ed. Don M. Wolfe. Ithaca, New York: Cornell University Press, 1948.

9. "Runaway." *Partisan Review,* 33 (Fall 1966), 574-82. (Excerpt from *The Confessions of Nat Turner.)*

10. "The Seduction of Leslie," *Esquire,* 86 (September 1976) 92-97.

11. "A Story About Christmas." *The Archive,* 58 (December 1944), 12-13.

12. "Sun on the River." *The Archive,* 58 (September 1944), 12-13.

13. "This Is My Daughter." *The Archive*, 59 (May 1946), 6-7, 20, 22, 24.

14. Typescript of an unpublished, untitled short novel. Washington, D.C.: The Library of Congress, Manuscript Division.

15. "Virginia: 1831." *Paris Review*, 9 (Winter 1966), 13-45. (Excerpt from *The Confessions of Nat Turner.)*

PLAYS

1. *Dead!* (a screenplay with John Phillips) *Esquire*, December 1973, pp. 161-68, 264, 266, 270, 274, 277, 278, 280, 282, 286, 288, 290.

2. *In the Clap Shack*
   New York: Random House, 1973.
   New York: New American Library/Plume, 1975.

ARTICLES AND REVIEWS
(Chronologically listed)

1. "Letter to an Editor." *Paris Review*, 1 (Spring 1953), 9-13.

2. "The Prevalence of Wonders." *Nation*, 2 May, 1953, pp. 370-71.

3. "The 'Paris Review'." *Harper's Bazaar*, 87 (August 1953), 122, 173.

4. "What's Wrong with the American Novel?" *American Scholar*, 24 (Autumn 1955), 464-503.

5. "If You Write for Television..." *New Republic*, 6 April 1959, p. 16.

6. "Introduction." *Best Short Stories from The Paris Review.* New York: E.P. Dutton & Co., Inc., 1959.

7. "Mrs. Aadland's Little Girl, Beverly." *Esquire,* November 1961, pp. 142, 189-91.

8. "The Death-in-Life of Benjamin Reid." *Esquire,* February 1962, pp. 114, 141-45.

9. "As He Lay Dead, a Bitter Grief." *Life,* July 20, 1962, pp. 39-42.

10. "The Aftermath of Benjamin Reid." *Esquire,* November 1962, pp. 79, 81, 158, 160, 164.

11. "Two Writers Talk It Over." *Esquire,* July 1963, pp. 57-59.

12. "Overcome." *New York Review of Books,* 26 September 1963, pp. 18-19.

13. "An Elegy for F. Scott Fitzgerald." *New York Review of Books,* 28 November 1963, pp. 1-3.

14. "The Habit." *New York Review of Books,* 26 December 1963, pp. 13-14.

15. "A Southern Conscience." *New York Review of Books,* 2 April 1964, p. 3.

16. "Tootsie Rolls." *New York Review of Books,* 14 May 1964, p. 8.

17. "MacArthur's Reminiscences." *New York Review of Books,* 8 October 1964, pp. 3-5.

18. "This Quiet Dust." *Harper's,* 230 (April 1965), 134-46.

19. "John Fitzgerald Kennedy...As We Remember Him." *High Fidelity,* 16 (January 1966), 38-40.

20. "Vice That Has No Name." *Harper's,* 236 (February 1968), 97-100.

21. "William Styron Replies." *Nation,* 22 April 1968, pp. 544-47.

22. "The Shade of Thomas Wolfe." *Harper's,* 236 (April 1968), 96-104.

23. "Oldest America." *McCall's*, July 1968, pp. 94, 123.

24. "My Generation." *Esquire*, October 1968, pp. 123-24.

25. "In the Jungle." *For Our Time.* Ed. Barry Gross. New York: Dodd & Mead Company, 1970.

26. "A Second Flowering." *The New York Times Book Review.* 6 May 1973, pp. 8, 10, 12, 14.

27. "Afterword." *The Long March* (Norwegian edition). *Mississippi Quarterly*, 28 (Spring 1975), 187-189.

28. "Introduction." *A Death in Canaan* by Joan Barthel. New York: E.P. Dutton and Co., Inc., 1976.

29. "Christchurch: An address delivered at Christchurch School (Virginia), May 28, 1975." Davidson, N.C.: Briarpatch Press, 1977.

WORKS IN PROGRESS

1. *The Way of the Warrior*, a novel about the Marine Corps. The title is a translation of bushido, the ancient code of the Japanese samurai.

2. *Sophie's Choice* (Tentative title), a novel about a woman who survives a Nazi concentration camp.

SECONDARY
SOURCES

BIBLIOGRAPHIES ON STYRON

1. Bryer, Jackson. "William Styron: A Bibliography." *The Achievement of William Styron.* Ed. Robert K. Morris and Irving Malin. Athens: The University of Georgia Press, 1975, pp. 242-277.

   This unannotated bibliography updates Bryer's and Marc Newman's list in *William Styron's "The Confessions of Nat Turner,"* edited by Melvin Friedman and Irving Malin. This is an extensive and exhaustive bibliography of both primary and secondary sources.

2. Bryer, Jackson and Marc Newman. "William Styron: A Bibliography." *William Styron's "The Confessions of Nat Turner": A Casebook.* Ed. Melvin Friedman and Irving Malin. Belmont, California: Wadsworth Publishing Co., 1970, pp. 258-280.

   A very thorough compilation. Jackson Bryer has added to this list in the recent collection of essays, *The Achievement of William Styron.* Particularly thorough with regard to book reviews.

3. Duff, John B. and Peter M. Mitchell, eds. *The Nat Turner Story: The Historical Event and the Modern Controversy.*

New York: Harper & Row, 1971, pp. 245-246.

> Selective and unannotated, this checklist in-
> cludes books related to the Nat Turner con-
> troversy. This is a good starting place for re-
> searchers interested in the controversy, though
> it is hardly a worthwhile endeavor to pursue
> the matter further.

4. Fossum, Robert H. *William Styron.* Grand Rapids, Michigan:
   Erdmans, 1968, pp. 47-48.

   > Selective and unannotated, this bibliography
   > contains some of the major criticisms of the
   > first three novels, but is of no help with *The
   > Confessions of Nat Turner.*

5. Friedman, Melvin. *William Styron.* Bowling Green, Ohio: Bowling Green University Popular Press, 1974, pp. 69-72.

   > Includes items useful in the preparation of
   > Friedman's pamphlet. Friedman recommends
   > that scholars consult the Bryer and Newman
   > bibliography in *William Styron's "The Con-
   > fessions of Nat Turner": A Critical Handbook,*
   > pp. 258-280.

6. Galloway, David D. "A William Styron Checklist." *The Absurd
   Hero in American Fiction.* Austin, Texas: University of
   Texas Press, 1966, pp. 203-210.

   > While not comprehensive, Galloway's check-
   > list is extensive.

7. Gerstenberger, Donna and George Hendrick. *The American
   Novel: A Checklist of Twentieth Century Criticism.* Chicago:
   The Swallow Press, Inc., 1970, pp. 322-325.

   > An excellent starting place for research. Con-
   > tains about ten articles each on Styron's four
   > novels, and seventeen items of general interest.
   > Not annotated.

8. Lawson, Lewis. "William Styron." *A Bibliographical Guide
   to the Study of Southern Literature.* Ed. Louis D. Rubin,

Jr. Baton Rouge: Louisiana State University Press, 1969, pp. 300-302.

Thirty items with an equitable distribution of Styron's four novels. This unannotated check-list provides an excellent overview of Styron's critical reception.

9. Leary, Lewis. *Articles on American Literature Appearing in Current Periodicals, 1950-1967.* Durham, N.C. Duke University Press, 1970, pp. 507-509.

This unannotated checklist contains forty-seven items but does not include the important Nat Turner items which can be found elsewhere.

10. Mackin, Cooper R. *William Styron.* Austin, Texas: Steck-Vaughn, 1969, pp. 39-43.

Mackin's pamphlet contains a selective, unannotated checklist of representative criticism, similar to the pamphlets of Friedman, Pearce, and Fossum.

11. Nevius, Blake. *The American Novel: Sinclair Lewis to the Present.* Northbrook, Illinois: AHM Publishing Corporation, 1970, pp. 90-91.

This selective bibliography in the Goldentree Series is brief and contains sources which are now dated. Contains no sources for *The Confessions of Nat Turner*, and is, therefore, of lesser value than other bibliographies.

12. Nigro, August J. "William Styron: Selection bibliographique." *La Revue des Lettres Modernes,* Nos. 157-61 (1967), 137-151.

Nigro assembled one of the earliest and best of the Styron bibliographies, containing both primary and secondary sources. Now dated because it was published before the considerable critical reactions to the Nat Turner book.

13. Pearce, Richard. *William Styron.* Minneapolis: University of Minnesota Press, 1971, pp. 44-47.

An unannotated, selected bibliography containing representative critical studies of Styron's works. Provides a good overview of Styron's critical reception.

14. Pearce, Richard. "William Styron." *American Writers.* Ed. Leonard Unger. New York: Charles Scribner's Sons, 1974, Vol. IV, pp. 117-119.

Unannotated checklist containing both primary and secondary sources. Essentially the same items found in Pearce's Minnesota Press Pamphlet *William Styron.*

15. Ratner, Marc. *William Styron.* New York: Twayne Publishers, 1973, pp. 153-166.

An excellent partially annotated bibliography containing primary and secondary sources. Ratner's bibliography, like his entire volume, is thorough and scholarly.

16. Schneider, H.W. "Two Bibliographies: Saul Bellow, William Styron." *Critique,* 3 (Summer 1960), 71-91.

Schneider's early bibliography is dated and of little use to scholars with access to other sources.

17. Walker, Warren S. *Twentieth-Century, Short Story Explication: Interpretations 1900-1966, Inclusive of Short Fiction Since 1800.* 2nd ed. Hamden, Connecticut: The Shoe String Press, Inc., 1968. (Supplement One to 2nd ed. 1967-1969, 1970.)

The Long March is classified as a short story in this collection. Styron's three major novels are, of course, excluded.

18. West, James L.W., III. *William Styron: A Descriptive Bibliography.* Boston: G.K. Hall, 1977.

This is a full-dress descriptive bibliography of the primary works. A thorough, authoritative treatment. West, a meticulous scholar, has gathered an impressive list of interviews with Styron and has contributed significantly to the body of professional attention to Styron and his writings.

BOOKS AND DOCTORAL DISSERTATIONS
ABOUT STYRON

When possible the annotations of doctoral dissertations contain summaries by the authors themselves. Order Numbers of dissertations from University Microfilms, Ann Arbor, Michigan, follow in parentheses.

1. Baumbach, Jonathan. "The Theme of Guilt and Redemption in The Post Second World War Novel." Ph.D. Dissertation, Stanford University, 1961, 244p. (61-4119)

   A thematic study of Warren's *All the King's Men*, Bellow's *The Victim*, Salinger's *Catcher in the Rye*, Ellison's *Invisible Man*, O'Connor's *Wise Blood*, Styron's *Lie Down in Darkness*, Malamud's *The Assistant*, and Wright Morris's, *Ceremony in Lone Tree*.

2. Cheshire, Ardner Randolph, Jr. "The Theme of Redemption in the Fiction of William Styron." Ph.D. Dissertation, Louisiana State University and Agricultural and Mechanical College, 1973, 114p. (74-18321)

   "In William Styron's fiction, redemption is primarily a matter of faith. In order to be saved, a man's faith in self or something beyond self must justify his existence....All of Styron's characters initially believe in a Winnie

the Pooh world of sweetness and light. Time
and experience, though, always destroy a character's childhood innocence—his naive faith
in an ordered and benevolent world."

3. Clarke, J.H., et al. *William Styron's Nat Turner: Ten Black
    Writer's Respond.* Boston: Beacon Press, 1968.

    Styron is personally called to task for his his-
    torical inaccuracies and for his psychological
    portrait of Nat Turner. For a detailed list of
    the contents see Clarke, J.H. as well as Will-
    iams, Ernest P., cited below.

4. Coale, Samuel Chase. "The Role of the South in the Fiction
    of William Faulkner, Carson McCullers, Flannery O'Connor,
    and William Styron." Ph.D. Dissertation, Brown University,
    1970, 388p. (71-13848)

    "The purpose of this thesis is to examine the
    changing role of the South in the fiction of
    William Faulkner, Carson McCullers, Flannery
    O'Connor, and William Styron and to explore
    the nature of the Southern imagination as re-
    vealed in the fiction....Styron's (South is) a
    self-indulgent world torn between existent
    guilt and existential awareness.

5. Corodimas, Peter Nicholas. "Guilt and Redemption in the No-
    vels of William Styron." Ph.D. Dissertation, The Ohio State
    University, 1971, 214p. (72-1519A)

    "Part of the technique of this study is to search
    out patterns of meaning, key scenes, and re-
    current images existing not only within each
    novel but also from one novel to the other....
    The novels do suggest an eschatological view,
    a hope that collective redemption will occur."

6. Duff, John B. and Peter M. Mitchell, eds. *The Nat Turner
    Story: The Historical Event and the Modern Controversy.*
    New York: Harper & Row, 1971.

    This book focuses on a subject that has lost
    its once lively flavor. Critics now view *The Con-*

fessions of Nat Turner as a work of art and
are not concerned with the book as history.

7. Firestone, Bruce M. "A Study of William Styron's Fiction."
Ph.D. Dissertation, The University of North Carolina at
Chapel Hill, 1975, 183p. (75-29022)

> "Past and present are constantly intermingled
> (in Styron's works), and much of the meaning
> of Styron's fiction derives from the interaction
> between what is being told and the process of
> telling." Louis D. Rubin, Jr., one of Styron's
> most faithful and complimentary critics, di-
> rected Firestone's thesis.

8. Fossum, R.H. *William Styron: A Critical Essay.* Grand Rapids,
Michigan: Erdmans, 1968.

> Finds that Styron's four novels "depict the
> spiritual vacuity of our age and the desperate
> measures men adopt in an effort to fill it." A
> very readable summary and critique of the no-
> vels in forty-seven pages.

9. Friedman, Melvin J. and August J. Nigro, eds. *Configuration
Critique de William Styron. La Revue des Lettres Modernes,*
Nos. 157-61 (1967).

> This is a collection of critical essays in French.
> *The Confessions of Nat Turner* is not included.
> Styron's French audience, popular and scholar-
> ly, is large.

10. Friedman, Melvin J. and Irving Malin, eds. *William Styron's
The Confessions of Nat Turner: A Casebook.* Belmont, California: Wadsworth Publishing Co., 1970.

> A collection of critical essays about *The Con-
> fessions of Nat Turner* primarily, but other
> Styron works are also discussed. A valuable
> volume.

11. Galloway, David Darryl. "The Absurd Hero in Contemporary
American Fiction: The Works of John Updike, William Styron, Saul Bellow, and J.D. Salinger." Ph.D. Dissertation,

State University of New York at Buffalo, 1962, 260 p. (62-05558)

"Because their examinations of absurdity have been particularly intense and thorough, John Updike, William Styron, Saul Bellow and J.D. Salinger are considered as representative of an absurd sensibility in American fiction. With Camus they share the belief that man must oppose an apparently meaningless universe, even though his demands for order and meaning make him absurd."

12. Goodley, Nancy Carter. "All Flesh is Grass: Despair and Affirmation in *Lie Down in Darkness.*" Ph. D. Dissertation, American University, 1975, 35p. (75-20509)

"Though it contains existential themes, *Lie Down in Darkness* is strongly affirmative and Christian—Paul Tillich's theology elucidates the novel's religious significance....Styron uses conventional literary forms and theological models, such as the meditation, the comic ending, and Soren Kierkegaard's three stages of existence to underscore his final message."

13. Hiers, John T. "Traditional Death Customs in Modern Southern Fiction." Ph.D. Dissertation, Emory University, 1974, 149p. (74-18385)

Deals with *Lie Down in Darkness.* "Death and funeral customs in modern Southern Fiction often become cultural tableaux for delineating healthful family and community relationships... and for maintaining vital regional and family traditions in a contemporary world of chaotic industrialization."

14. Hoerchner, Susan J. " 'I Have to Keep The Two Things Separate': Polarity in Women in the Contemporary American Novel." Ph.D. Dissertation, Emory University, 1974, 231p. (74-10287)

"In the contemporary American novel the social woman denies the flesh simply because she fears or hates the body. As a result of this moral bankruptcy she becomes a destructive force....Like William Styron's Helen Loftis in *Lie Down in Darkness*, she may wreak havoc with people in her immediate environment."

15. Hux, Samuel Holland. "American Myth and Existential Vision: The Indigenous Existentialism of Mailer, Bellow, Styron, and Ellison." Ph.D. Dissertation, The University of Connecticut, 1965, 340p. (66-857)

   "The indigenous existentialism of these writers, and its adumbrations in earlier writers, is in part a response to the collapse of one of two native myths." Discusses the "American Eden" and "the myth created by the imagination of the South."

16. Kime, Benna Kay. "A Critical Study of the Technique of William Styron." Ph.D. Dissertation, Tulane University, 1971. 168 p. (71-27289)

   "This dissertation is primarily concerned with the sheer technical virtuosity of William Styron's best work. Attention is concentrated on Styron's early short stories and on *Lie Down in Darkness* and *The Confessions of Nat Turner*. The two novels have been chosen because they illustrate one of the principal characteristics of the modern novel: the development of experimental third and first person narrative techniques."

17. Lang, John Douglas. "William Styron: The Christian Imagiination." Ph.D. Dissertation, Stanford University, 1975, 414p. (76-5754)

   "Without appealing to Christian dogma as final revelation, Styron nevertheless suggests that the essentially human depends upon a concrete *imitatio Christi*. Consequently, the tenents of Christianity become the critic's most valuable heuristic device for a fuller appreciation of Styron's writing."

18. Leon, Philip Wheeler. "Idea and Technique in the Novels of William Styron." Ph.D. Dissertation, Peabody College, 1974, 259 p. (75-12449)

> Examines each of Styron's novels for its distinctive "idea"—central metaphor, dominant image, controlling theme—as conveyed by Styron's "technique"—the use of artistic devices.

19. Luttrell, William. "Tragic and Comic Modes in Twentieth-Century American Literature: William Styron and Joseph Heller." Ph.D. Dissertation, Bowling Green State University, 1969, 145 p. (69-21645)

> "William Styron and Joseph Heller offer spiritual paradigms of the novel of victimization. Their central characters are subject to disintegrating forces over which they appear to have little control."

20. Mackin, Cooper, R. *William Styron.* Austin, Texas: Steck-Vaughn, 1969.

> A critical assessment of Styron's fiction with emphasis on social immediacy and consummate artistry of *The Confessions of Nat Turner.* This pamphlet draws parallels between Styron's heroes as Southern rebels. A readable overview.

21. Mewshaw, Michael Francis. "Thematic and Stylistic Problems in the Work of William Styron." Ph.D. Dissertation, University of Virginia, 1970, 201 p. (71-06662)

> "This paper is an attempt to examine Styron's work objectively, with particular attention to the themes and elements of style which emerge in the course of the four books."

22. Mills, Eva Bamberger. "The Development of William Styron's Artistic Consciousness: A Study of the Relationship Between Life and Work." Ph.D. Dissertation, University of Cincinnati, 1976, 189 p. (76-25507)

> Styron believes that, "by critically evaluating his own past and past events, both personal

and historical, he, like so many of his characters, can come to a better understanding of
himself and of reality and, as a result, be in a
better position to carry out his mission as an
artist." Mills provides an extra-literary dimension to the Styron scholarship.

23. Morgan, Henry Grady, Jr. "The World as a Prison: A Study
     of the Novels of William Styron." Ph.D. Dissertation, Uni-
     versity of Colorado, 1973, 183p. (73-23283)

     "The four novels of William Styron reflect a
     world that is at its core a prison. This im-
     prisonment is the basic condition of mankind,
     and from it there is no escape. What each of
     the protagonists in the novels must do is come
     to a recognition of the fact of his bondage and
     come to some accord with that fact: he must
     find a *raison d'etre* even within the confines
     of that bondage."

24. Morris, Robert K. and Irving Malin. *The Achievement of Will-
     iam Styron.* Athens: The University of Georgia Press, 1975.

     The most recent collection of essays. Contains
     two excellent interviews with Styron, particu-
     larly the one by editor Morris. Most of the
     articles have appeared previously, but this
     collection is a representative sample of the
     critical activity surrounding Styron. For a
     perceptive review of this book see James L.W.
     West III, "The Breadth, Depth of an Oeuvre,"
     The Roanoke Times, 9 November 1975,
     "Books."

25. Nigro, Augustine John, Jr. "William Styron and the Adamic
     Tradition." Ph.D. Dissertation, The University of Maryland,
     1964, 258p. (64-11105)

     "William Styron's *Lie Down in Darkness*, *The
     Long March*, and *Set This House on Fire* are
     novels emerging from and contributing to a
     tradition in American fiction variously defined
     as 'the American Adam', 'the American Dream,'
     and 'Paradise (to be) Regained.' "

26. O'Connell, Shaun Vincent. "The Contexts of William Styron's *The Confessions of Nat Turner.*" Ph.D. Dissertation, University of Massachusetts, 1970, 342p. (70-21117)

> "This work examines the contexts of William Styron's *The Confessions of Nat Turner:* aesthetic, historical, cultural."

27. Ownbey, Ray Wilson. "To Choose Being: The Function of Order and Disorder in William Styron's Fiction." Ph.D. Dissertation, University of Utah, 1972, 135p. (72-23273)

> In his four novels "Styron has shown us various attempts to establish personal order, to 'be,' and the sex, religion, and violence are used as a vivid means with which to illustrate those attempts." Ownbey's dissertation, written in slangy, unscholarly style, is a superficial treatment. Not worth consulting.

28. Pearce, Richard. *William Styron.* Minneapolis: University of Minnesota Press, 1971.

> Well unified pamphlet which puts *The Long March* as central thematically in Styron's career. As with so many pamphlets in this series, space limitations prohibit an extensive examination of the primary sources.

29. Peterson, Sandra M. "The View from the Gallows: The Criminal Confession in American Literature." Ph.D. Dissertation, Northwestern University, 1972, 135p. (72-32540)

> "This discussion uses the criminal confession as a touchstone with which to examine the relationships between man, society, and a divine order in American literature. It considers Puritan confessional literature and four American novels: *The Scarlet Letter, Billy Budd, An American Tragedy,* and *The Confessions of Nat Turner.*"

30. Ratner, Marc. *William Styron.* New York: Twayne Publishers, 1973.

A critical and biographical overview consisting mainly of previously published articles in various scholarly journals. In the preface Ratner says Styron, "More than any of his contemporaries in American fiction, with the possible exception of John Hawkes, approximates the poetic power of Herman Melville and William Faulkner."

31. Scott, James Burton. "The Individual and Society: Norman Mailer Versus William Styron." Ph.D. Dissertation, Syracuse University, 1964, 169p. (65-03436)

Contrasts Styron's first three novels with Mailer's first three. "The novels are examined for evidence that reveals how their authors feel about the interrelationships between individuals and the society in which they live."

32. Strine, Mary Susan. "The Novel as Rhetorical Act: An Interpretation of the Major Fiction of William Styron." Ph.D. Dissertation, University of Washington, 1972, 186p. (73-13885)

"The novels of William Styron are placed within the historico-cultural perspective of a central misguiding metaphor for the American cultural experience, the Adamic Myth which holds a New World individual to be inherently innocent and boundless in self-determining potential."

33. Swanson, William Joseph. "William Styron, Eloquent Protestant." Ed.D Dissertation, University of Northern Colorado, 1972, 176 p. (73-00316)

"This study attempts to demonstrate that William Styron is not only a protest writer, but an 'unconventional' protest writer: one who employs the rhetoric of the traditionalist (rhetoric that is characterized by long, carefully constructed sentences, poetic diction and copious literary allusions.)"

CHAPTERS AND REFERENCES TO STYRON
IN BOOKS

1. Aldridge, John W. "The Society of Three Novels." *In Search of Heresy*. New York: McGraw-Hill Book Company, 1956, pp. 126-148.

   Aldridge describes Styron as "the most accomplished member of the younger group of Southern novelists....Behind Milton's father-guilt and incest-guilt is the whole Southern blood-guilt" of *Lie Down in Darkness*.

2. Aldridge, John W. "William Styron and the Derivative Imagination." *Time to Murder and Create: The Contemporary Novel in Crisis*. New York: McKay, 1966.

   "In everything he has done up to now he has managed to be acceptable and not sounding so familiar as to seem entirely unoriginal." Aldridge is particularly disparaging of *Set This House on Fire* because of its "self-obsessed excavation and examination of nuance."

3. Aldridge, John W. *The Devil in the Fire*. New York: Harper & Row, 1972.

   Reprint of "William Styron and the Derivative Imagination" from *Time to Murder and Create*.

4. Allen, Walter. *The Modern Novel.* New York: E.P. Dutton, 1965.

> Styron is included with Bowles, Capote, McCullers, Buechner, and O'Connor in what Allen calls the "gothic, Southern" mode of American writers. Allen calls *Lie Down in Darkness* "an attempt at what might be called Freudian tragedy made very nearly successful by the power of the poetry—descriptive, lyrical, elegiac—that clothes it; and it is also a formal achievement on a high plane of intention."

5. Baumbach, Jonathan. "Paradise Lost: The Novels of William Styron." *The Landscape of Nightmare.* New York: New York University Press, 1965, pp. 123-137.

> An intensive treatment of *Lie Down in Darkness.* Baumbach says the novel remains "the most ostentatiously talented first novel of its period. The prodigious brilliance of its performance resides in the richness and grace of the language and the intricate, almost impossible complexity of the structure." Baumbach's dissertation (Stanford, 1961) includes a treatment of Styron's first novel.

6. Bradbury, John M. *Renaissance in the South: A Critical History of the Literature, 1920-1960.* Chapel Hill: University of North Carolina Press, 1963.

> Styron "represents best the new semiexistential leaning of the World War II generation. Styron bursts with talent."

7. Bridgman, Richard. *The Colloquial Style in America.* New York: Oxford University Press, 1966, p. 13.

> Styron's writing "indulges in that public oratory we habitually associate with the Southern politician." Not an extensive treatment.

8. Brodin, Pierre. *Presences contemporaines. Ecrivains Americains D'aujourdi'hui.* Paris: N.E.D., editeur, 1964, pp. 169-177.

An overview of Styron's works, exclusive of
Nat Turner. Brodin calls Styron the most Flau-
bertian of contemporary American writers
and the writer most apt to be appreciated in
France. Scholars interested in Styron's success
in France will find this early assessment valuable.

9.   Bryant, Jerry H. *The Open Decision: The Contemporary
     American Novel and Its Intellectual Background.* New York:
     The Free Press, 1970, pp. 52, 71, 264-68, 282.

A brief criticism of *Set This House on Fire*
contends that Styron sees the problem of human life as the "danger of losing faith in the
obscure and hidden foundations of our being
and the consequent need to find the courage to
restore that faith."

10. Burgess, Anthony. *The Novel Now: A Guide to Contemporary
     Fiction.* New York: W.W. Norton & Co., Inc., 1967, p. 54.

"*The Long March* deals brilliantly with a familiar American military theme—the enmity
between temperamentally opposed officers,
the self-destructive stoicism that follows on
defiant obedience to a tyrannous discipline.
We have seen it often presented, but rarely
with such compressed eloquence." Burgess, a
perceptive critic, writes well about Styron.

11. Chapsal, Madeleine. *Quinze ecrivains.* Paris: Juillard, 1963.

A reprint of an interview with Styron from
L'Express, no. 560 (8 March 1962), 26-27.

12. Clarke, John H., ed. *William Styron's Nat Turner: Ten Black
     Writers Respond.* Boston: Beacon, 1968.

These ten writers attack Styron on several
levels: social, racial, psychological, historical.
The individual chapters follow:
Bennett, L. "Nat's Last White Man." pp. 3-16.
Hairston, L. "William Styron's Nat Turner—Rogue-Nigger."
     pp. 68-72.

Hamilton, C.V. "Our Nat Turner and William Styron's Creation." pp. 73-78.

Harding, V. "You've Taken My Nat and Gone." pp. 23-33.

Kaiser, E. "The Failure of William Styron." pp. 50-65.

Killens, J.O. "The Confessions of Willie Styron." pp. 34-44.

Poussaint, A.F. "The Confessions of Nat Turner and the Dilemma of William Styron." pp. 17-22.

Thelwell, M. "Back with the Wind: Mr. Styron and the Reverend Turner." pp. 79-91.

Williams, J.A. "The Manipulation of History and of Fact: An Ex-Southerner's Apologist Tract for Slavery and the Life of Nat Turner; or, William Styron's Faked Confessions." pp. 45-49.

13. Cowley, Malcolm. *A Second Flowering: Works and Days of The Lost Generation.* New York: The Viking Press, 1973, p. 237.

> World War II was "not a lucky war for the younger writers" such as Bellow, Mailer, Styron, Jarrell, and others. Scholars will find this volume useful in providing a historical perspective for Styron's early work.

14. Cowley, Malcolm. *The Literary Situation.* New York: The Viking Press, 1954, pp. 69, 82.

> Describes Styron's "brilliant" first novel's heroine as "seeking for a lost father image." Peyton Loftis of *Lie Down in Darkness* cannot succeed in her marriage because of the destructive influence of her father.

15. Davis, Robert G. "The American Individualist Tradition: Bellow and Styron." *The Creative Present.* Ed. Norma Balakian and Charles Simmons. New York: Doubleday & Company, Inc., 1963, pp. 111-141.

> Discusses the first three novels. Styron and Bellow make life seem empty by removing their characters from ordinary society with its ordinary responsibilities. The lack of a treatment of Styron's *Nat Turner* detracts from the value of this dated criticism.

16. Detweiler, Robert. "William Styron and the Courage to Be." *Four Spiritual Crises in Mid-Century American Fiction.* Gainesville, Florida: University of Florida Press, 1964, pp. 6-13.

    Set This House on Fire bears similarities to Paul Tillich's religious consciousness. A comparison of Tillich and Styron. A narrowly focused treatment depending upon a religious approach.

17. Duberman, Martin B. *The Uncompleted Past.* New York: Dutton, 1971.

    A historian likes *The Confessions of Nat Turner,* saying the historical inaccuracies are petty and do not disrupt the artistry of the novel.

18. Edminston, Susan and Linda D. Cirino. *Literary New York: A History and Guide.* Boston: Houghton Mifflin Co., 1976.

    A survey of literary activity in New York with discussions of Agee, Bontemps, Capote, Clemens, Ellison, Faulkner, McCullers, Poe, Styron, Wolfe, Wright, and other Southerners with New York connnections.

19. Eisinger, Chester E. *Fiction of the Forties.* Chicago: The University of Chicago Press, 1965, p. 370.

    Styron maintains, along with Jean Stafford, Ralph Ellison, and others that the novel is not dead.

20. Finkelstein, Sidney. "Cold War, Religious Revival and Family Alienation: William Styron, J.D. Salinger, and Edward Albee." *Existentialism and Alienation in American Literature.* New York: International Publishers, 1965, pp. 211-242.

    Summarizes Styron's first three novels. Says Styron excels Faulkner in *Lie Down in Darkness.* Despite that implausible statement, the book aids in understanding Styron and his contemporaries.

21. French, Warren. *The Fifties: Fiction, Poetry, Drama.* Deland,

Florida: Everett/Edwards, Inc., 1970, p. 13.

> Briefly mentions Styron's *Lie Down in Darkness* as a product of the "seemingly indefatigable South." Styron is one of a group of "intense young writers moved by spiritual distress to a bizarre mixture of sentimentalism and cynicism." Use your time other than in consulting this book.

22. Friedman, Melvin J. "William Styron." *The Politics of Twenieth-Century Novelists.* Ed. George A. Panichas. New York: Apollo Editions, 1974.

> Reprinted in *William Styron* (Bowling Green, Ohio: Bowling Green University Popular Press, 1974, pp. 37-53.) A good review of the Nat Turner controversy. Friedman contends that Styron's novel is the natural outgrowth of his personal, social, and political views. The novel is part of an overall liberal stance reflected in Styron's non-fiction writing.

23. Fuller, Edmund. *Books With Men Behind Them.* New York: Random House, 1962, pp. 9-10.

> *Set This House on Fire* revealed a major step in the maturing of Styron's considerable powers.

24. Galloway, David D. *The Absurd Hero in American Fiction: Updike, Styron, Bellow, Salinger.* Austin: University of Texas Press, 1966, pp. 65-81.

> A treatment of Styron's major fiction, exclusive of *The Confessions of Nat Turner:* "Characters and story are of immense importance to Styron ....For all his psychoanalytic inclinations, Styron tends to see his characters as figures from a Greek drama, as bored, tormented, and destined souls, in essence far removed from the aid of the analyst." This work is a re-write of Galloway's dissertation (SUNY-Buffalo, 1962).

25. Gayle, Addison, Jr. *The Way of the New World: The Black*

Novel in America. Garden City, New York: Anchor Press/ Doubleday, 1975, pp. 224, 231, 234-37, 248.

An attack on Styron's *The Confessions of Nat Turner:* "It is the product of a white man lacking the courage to confront history as revealed fact; one who must, instead, deal with it as fable and myth in an attempt to sanction the image of the 'good, loyal darky.' "

26. Geismar, Maxwell. "William Styron: The End of Innocence." *American Moderns: From Rebellion to Conformity.* New York: Hill and Wang, 1958, pp. 239-50.

Focuses on *The Long March* as "a propaganda tale, embodying that 'individual' protest which William Styron believes to be so hopeless today."

27. Geismar, Maxwell. "The Shifting Illusion: Dream and Fact." in *American Dreams, American Nightmares,* ed. David Madden. Carbondale and Edwardsville: Southern Illinois University Press, 1970.

"Despite all the critical acclaim for William Styron's *Confessions of Nat Turner,* in 1967, this very talented artist has descended to the level of a commercial best-seller writer and a romantic pseudo-historian."

28. Genovese, Eugene D. "William Styron before the People's Court." *In Red and Black: Marxian Explorations in Southern and Afro-American History.* New York: Pantheon Books, 1972, pp. 200-217.

A defense of Styron's fictional treatment of Nat Turner.

29. Gossett, Louise Y. "The Cost of Freedom." *Violence in Recent Southern Fiction.* Durham, N.C.: Duke University Press, 1965, pp. 117-131.

"The conditions of freedom for man within institutions and within himself occupy William Styron. Whether rebelling against oppressive authority or craving the direction of kindly authority, his characters are trying to establish a creative relationship between freedom and discipline." Gossett's excellent book is one of the standard, authoritative secondary sources. An invaluable reference for students of literature.

30. Gross, Theodore L. *The Heroic Ideal in American Literature.* New York: The Free Press, 1971, p. 178.

"William Styron cannot write a good book on Nat Turner without being attacked far beyond legitimate literary terms. Criticism of black literature is so often banal because it is so chauvinistic—blacks praise blacks and whites are afraid to use the criteria they would naturally apply to other literature." An intriguing premise amply supported.

31. Handy, William J. *Modern Fiction: A Formalist Approach.* Carbondale and Edwardsville: Southern Illinois University Press, 1971, p. 119.

"The writers of the last ten years present a new world and a new problem: in the novels of Salinger, Bellow, Styron, Roth, and Malamud, the dominant theme is man's struggle to discover himself, not merely his psychological self, but his ethical self and his religious self." Very little detail about Styron; an overview of Styron's contemporaries.

32. Harte, Barbara and Carolyn Riley, eds. *200 Contemporary Authors.* Detroit: Gale Research Company 1969.

A biographical account, plus an overview of Styron's work. Contains brief excerpts of criticism.

33. Hartt, Julian N. *Lost Image of Man.* Baton Rouge: Louisiana State University Press, 1963.

A key to understanding *Lie Down in Darkness* is that Milton Loftis never escaped the domination of his father. Helen's father endowed

her with sexual frigidity. The theme of the
father is central to Peyton's "radically con-
fused love."

34. Hassan, Ihab. *Contemporary American Literature, 1945-1972.*
New York: Frederick Ungar Publishing Co., 1973.

> "(Styron's) work, brilliant in parts, shifting
> from rhetoric to sudden poetry, dramatically
> rich, seeks between violence and ambiguity
> some definition of personal integrity. The
> search often fails because Styron seems to
> lack a felt attitude toward life, a distinctive
> power of evaluation." Hassan's writings about
> American fiction are scholarly and trustworthy.
> His assessments inform and illuminate.

35. Hassan, Ihab. "Encounter With Necessity: Styron, Swados,
Mailer." *Radical Innocence: Studies in the Contemporary
Novel.* Princeton, N.J.: Princeton University Press, 1961,
pp. 124-134.

> An extensive examination of *Lie Down in
> Darkness.* Hassan says that *Lie Down in Dark-
> ness* is a "brilliant formal accomplishment....
> This is a story of infidelity, of vengeful love,
> blocked, hurt, and perverted, of adults who
> can never escape their childhood." In all three
> of Styron's novels he "reveals a brooding ima-
> gination, sometimes obsessive, and a dark gift
> of poetry."

36. Hassan, Ihab. "The Pattern of Fictional Experience." *Modern
American Fiction.* Ed. A. Walton Litz. New York: Oxford
University Press, 1963, pp. 315-334.

> Reprinted from *Radical Innocence.* The existen-
> tial experience is not diminished by history as
> shown by the works of Ellison, Mailer, Styron,
> Bowles, and Bellow.

37. Hassan, Ihab. "William Styron." *Encyclopedia of World Literature in the 20th Century.* Ed. Wolfgang Bernard Fleisch-
mann. New York: Frederick Ungar Publishing Co., 1971.
Vol. III.

A biographical and critical overview. Brief but valuable for the beginning Styron scholar.

38. Hays, Peter L. *The Limping Hero: Grotesques in Literature.* New York: New York University Press, 1971.

    Captain Mannix of *The Long March* is, like many "limping heroes," related to tragic heroes from classical and biblical literature.

39. Henderson, Stephen. "Survival Motion: A Study of the Black Writer and the Black Revolution in America." *The Militant Black Writer.* Stephen Henderson and Mercer Cook. Madison, Wisconsin: The University of Wisconsin Press, 1969.

    Henderson's comments on *The Confessions of Nat Turner* are vitriolic: "One can be fairly certain that the next white writer will think twice before presuming to interpret the Black Experience." Poorly written, vindictive, and puerile.

40. Hirsch, E.D. *Validity in Interpretation.* New Haven, Connecticut: Yale University Press, 1967, pp. 148, 149, 254.

    "The younger American writers coming on the scene—Bowles, Eudora Welty, Carson Mc-Cullers, Tennessee Williams, Saul Bellow, Truman Capote, Vance Bourjaily, William Styron, Norman Mailer, James Baldwin, Ralph Ellison, *et. al.*—were specialists in loneliness, anxiety, hatred, and terror." No detailed remarks on Styron.

41. Hoffman, Frederick J. "The Cure of 'Nothing': The Fiction of William Styron." *Frontiers of American Culture.* Eds. Ray B. Browne, Richard H. Crowder, Virgil L. Lokke, and William T. Stafford. Lafayette, Indiana: Purdue University Studies, 1968.

    See next entry for annotation.

42. Hoffman, Frederick J. "William Styron: The Metaphysical Hurt." *The Art of Southern Fiction.* Carbondale and Ed-

wardsville, Illinois: Southern Illinois University Press, 1966, pp. 144-164.

> "The pathos of his creatures, when it is not directly the result of organizational absurdity, comes from a psychological failure, a 'confusion,' a situation in which the character, trying to meet an awkward human situation, makes it worse and (almost invariably) retreats clumsily or despairingly from it."

43. Holman, C. Hugh. *The Roots of Southern Writing*. Athens: University of Georgia Press, 1972, p. 125.

> Styron is part of the group of writers who are concerned with the reality of the past in the present and with the nature of time. *Lie Down in Darkness* exemplifies this theme.

44. Holman, C. Hugh. *The Immoderate Past: The Southern Writer and History*. Athens: The University of Georgia Press, 1976.

> Deals with the southern writer's preoccupation with history, concentrating on representative novelists from three major periods—antebellum, post Civil War, and post 1930. Discusses Styron, Simms, Glasgow, Heyward, Young, Tate, Mitchell, Walker, Warren. Holman, a co-editor of *Southern Literary Journal*, is a faultless scholar whose observations merit attention.

45. Hubbell, Jay B. *Who Are the Major American Writers?* Durham, N.C.: Duke University Press, 1972.

> Styron is included in a list of the twenty authors selected by "200 prominent authors, critics, and editors" as being one of the "Best Writers of Fiction." Styron's *Lie Down in Darkness* is listed as one of "The Twenty Best Works of Fiction." Poll taken by *Book Week* for its September 26, 1965 issue.

46. Jones, Howard Mumford and Richard M. Ludwig. *Guide to American Literature and its Backgrounds Since 1890*. 3rd

ed. Cambridge, Massachusetts: Harvard University Press, 1964, pp. 194, 199.

Lie Down in Darkness is included in a list of "Novels in the Period of the Cold War." *The Long March* is listed with "The Literature of World War II." The latter novel actually is set in America during the Korean War and deals with marine reservists recalled to duty.

47. Kaufman, Walter. "Tragedy vs. History: *The Confessions of Nat Turner.*" *Tragedy and Philosophy.* New York: Doubleday, 1968.

An exploration of Styron's reshaping of historical facts to create a fictional hero of tragic dimensions.

48. Kazin, Alfred. "The Alone Generation." *Contemporaries.* Boston: Little, Brown, 1962, pp. 214-216.

Briefly discusses Styron in the context of post-World War II fiction. Not detailed.

49. Kazin, Alfred. *Bright Book of Life: American Novelists and Storytellers from Hemingway to Mailer.* Boston: Little, Brown and Company, 1973, pp. 227-229; 290-291.

Contains a lucid explanation of the social forces which rebelled against Styron's fictional portrayal of Nat Turner. One of the better treatments of this subject.

50. Klein, Marcus. *After Alienation: American Novels in Mid-Century.* New York: Books for Libraries, 1964.

Cites Styron as a writer who is worthy of estimation. No amplification.

51. Kort, W.A. "*The Confessions of Nat Turner* and the Dynamic Revolution." *Shriven Selves: Religious Problems in Recent American Fiction.* Philadelphia: Fortress Press, 1972, pp. 116-140.

In *The Confessions of Nat Turner* Styron's principal interest "seems to lie in the resources

of confessional fiction and in the phenomenon
of a revolutionary act." The religious approach
does not allow the full range of possible literary
treatments available to the critic.

52. Kostelanetz, Richard, ed. *On Contemporary Literature.* New
York: Avon Books, 1964, pp. 597-606.

Reprint of Ihab Hassan's "Encounter with Necessity" from *Radical Innocence.* Princeton,
N.J.: Princeton University Press, 1961, pp.
124-134.

53. Kuehl, John. *Write and Re-Write.* New York: Meredith Press,
1967, pp. 294-308.

Contains photocopies of part of Styron's holo-
graph manuscript of *The Long March,* showing
the author's revisions. Interesting for textual
scholars and those intrigued with the process of
composition.

54. Ludwig, Jack. *Recent American Novelists.* Minneapolis: University of Minnesota Press, 1962, p. 34.

"Styron's novels are peopled by well-heeled,
beer-guzzling, suddenly idea-stricken 'Gentlemen C' party boys who use their college education rather well." One of the Minnesota series
pamphlets and therefore limited in scope.

55. Lytle, Andrew. *Hero With the Private Parts.* Baton Rouge:
Louisiana State University Press, 1966, pp. 50-55.

"A writer who started out well, William Styron, has a recent book, *Set This House on Fire,*
which could serve as an example for the failure
of the first person view. It is a long, discursive
book, and in the two hundred thousand words
of impression, much does not bear directly
upon the action."

56. Mailer, Norman. *Advertisements for Myself.* New York: New
American Library, 1960.

Styron's sometime enemy accuses him of slickness. Mailer's personal and literary insecurity cloud his vision.

57. Matthiessen, Peter and George Plimpton. "William Styron." *Writers at Work: The "Paris Review" Interviews*. Ed. Malcolm Cowley. New York: The Viking Press, 1959.

An early interview in which Styron discusses *Lie Down in Darkness* and himself. He eschews the "Southern" label, and discusses his view of contemporary fiction.

58. Meeker, Richard K. "The Youngest Generation of Southern Fiction Writers." *Southern Writers*. Ed. Rinaldo C. Simonini, Jr. Freeport, N.Y.: Books for Libraries, Inc., 1964, pp. 162-191.

Explores *Lie Down in Darkness* as an example of the "new" Southern fiction. "The young Southern writer is interested in the past not to show the pastness of the present, but to show the presentness of the present." Current readers may find the book dated in its conclusions.

59. Millgate, Michael. *American Social Fiction: James to Cozzens*. New York: Barnes & Noble, Inc., 1964, p. 201.

"Some of the best among recent American novelists, notably Saul Bellow and William Styron," seem to take society "more or less for granted," thereby eliminating self-conscious attempts to relate to that society. Deals in generalities with regard to Styron.

60. Morse, J. Mitchell. *The Irrelevant English Teacher*. Philadelphia: Temple University Press, 1972.

An extremely hostile criticism of Styron and *The Confessions of Nat Turner*. Says the novel has "no value at all...as a work of art it doesn't exist." Morse's "evidence" is superficial, petty, and unjustified.

61. Mudrick, Marvin. "Mailer and Styron." *On Culture and Lit-*

erature. New York: Horizon Press, 1970, pp. 176-199. Reprinted from *Hudson Review*, 17 (1967), 346-366.

> Deals with the later books of these two novelists as well as *The Naked and the Dead* and *Lie Down in Darkness*. "These two are derivative, and at their best merely vehement books. Both Mailer and Styron desire fame and power, or to be accepted by the famous and powerful—desires which are inimical to good fiction."

62. Nyren, Dorothy, ed. *A Library of Literary Criticism*. New York: Frederick Ungar Publishing Co., 1964.

> A selection of criticism, exclusive of *The Confessions of Nat Turner*.

63. O'Conner, William Van. "John Updike and William Styron: The Burden of Talent." *Contemporary American Novelists*. Ed. Harry T. Moore. Carbondale and Edwardsville, Illinois: Southern Illinois University Press, 1964, pp. 205-221.

> Examines *Lie Down in Darkness* and *Set This House on Fire*. Says Styron is a writer of "enormous talent in search of a subject."

64. Olderman, Raymond. *Beyond the Waste Land: A Study of the American Novel in the Nineteen-Sixties*. New Haven: Yale University Press, 1972, pp. 14, 95, 177.

> "In the novel of the fifties, chaos of any kind provoked our greatest terror—in Bellow, Ellison, or Styron chaos always signified the breakdown of the human spirit in the face of an orderless world." There is no sustained examination of Styron's work.

65. Pearce, Richard. "William Styron." *American Writers*. Ed. Leonard Unger. New York: Charles Scribner's Sons, 1964.

> Excellent overview of Styron and his work. Underscores the social factors which separate Styron from the earlier era of writers such as Faulkner.

66. Poirer, Richard. *The Performing Self: Compositions and De-*

Compositions in the Language of Contemporary Life. New York: Oxford University Press, 1971, pp. 5-6.

In *The Confessions of Nat Turner* Styron is unable to give a convincing voice to Nat which would be "distinguishable from that of the elegantly rhetorical narrator." An interesting view which will appeal to linguists.

67. Riley, Carolyn, ed. "William Styron." *Contemporary Literary Criticism.* Detroit: Gale Research Co., 1975. (Vol. I, pp. 329-331; Vol. III, pp. 472-475.)

Contains representative selections from substantial criticisms of Styron's work. A valuable overview and time-saving reference for the beginning Styron scholar.

68. Rubin, Louis D. Jr. *The Comic Imagination in American Literature.* New Brunswick, N.J.: Rutgers University Press, 1973, pp. 375, 383.

Styron's novels offer "fictions that embody an intelligible theme in some formal arrangement of coherent actions involving fully realized characters."

69. Rubin, Louis D. Jr. *The Curious Death of the Novel: Essays in American Literature.* Baton Rouge: Louisiana State University Press, 1967.

A substantial number of excellent writers, Styron among them, belie the idea that the novel as art form no longer exists. Calls Styron "the most brilliant young writer since World War II."

70. Rubin, Louis D. Jr. "William Styron." *Contemporary Novelists.* Ed. James Vinson. New York: St. Martin's Press, 1972, pp. 1201-1203.

Contains biographical precis, brief summaries of plots, and critical reception of Styron's novels. Styron's works show "a profound belief in the reality of the past as importantly affecting present behavior."

71. Rubin, Louis D. Jr. "William Styron: Notes on a Southern Writer in Our Time." *The Faraway Country.* Seattle: University of Washington Press, 1963, pp. 185-230.

    Discusses Styron's first three novels as illustrating the changing assumptions and attitudes from one generation of Southern writers to the next.

72. Rubin, Louis D. Jr. "William Styron and Human Bondage: *The Confessions of Nat Turner.*" *The Sounder Few: Essays from the "Hollins Critic."* Ed. R.H.W. Dillard, George Garrett, and John Rees Moore. Athens: University of Georgia Press, 1971.

    "Nat, a human being, rebels because he is deprived by his society of the right to love and be loved."

73. Rubin, Louis D. Jr. *The Writer in the South: Studies in a Literary Community.* Athens: University of Georgia Press, 1972, p. 3.

    "Anyone who has read (Styron's) account of how the subject of the Nat Turner insurrection came to possess his imagination will not be misled by any effort on Styron's part to pretend that as an author he has not felt a strong compulsion to 'tell about the South.' "

74. Rubin, Louis D. Jr. and John Rees Moore. *The Idea of an American Novel.* New York: Thomas Y. Crowell Co., 1961, pp. 368-370.

    Excerpt reprinted from *Writers at Work: The "Paris Review" Interviews.* See entry 57 (Matthiessen), this section.

75. Rubin, Louis D. Jr. and Robert D. Jacobs, eds. *South: Modern Southern Literature and Its Cultural Setting.* Westport, Connecticut: Greenwood Press, Inc., 1974. (Reprint of 1961 edition.)

    Mentions Styron briefly in a checklist of Southern writers. This work appears too early in Styron's career to include substantial criticism.

76. Scott, Nathan A. Jr. *Three American Moralists: Mailer, Bellow, Trilling.* Notre Dame: University of Notre Dame Press, 1973, pp. 71, 103.

> "It would be silly to postulate the death of a medium whose characteristic practitioners today are people so talented as John Barth, Bernard Malamud, William Styron, John Hawkes, Norman Mailer, and Thomas Pynchon."

77. Sheed, Wilfrid. *The Morning After.* New York: Farrar, Straus and Giroux, Inc., 1971, pp. 83-89.

> Discussing *The Confessions of Nat Turner*, Sheed maintains that "one grows frustrated at times watching the author squeeze his own excellent prose into this whalebone of rhetoric: but he gets off some fine phrases, and the writing in fact carries one over a good deal of wasteland." Sheed demonstrates that he is a better reviewer than he is a literary scholar.

78. Simonini, R.C. Jr. *Southern Writers: Appraisals in Our Time.* Charlottesville: The University Press of Virginia, 1964, pp. 187-188.

> A brief summary of *The Long March.* "Styron draws an ironic contrast between the free will allowed men in the outside world and the utter submission to authority required in the Marines."

79. Skaggs, Merrill Maguire. *The Folk of Southern Fiction.* Athens: The University of Georgia Press, 1972, p. 219.

> Cites Styron among "the most important American writers of fiction in this century." No amplification.

80. Solotaroff, Theodore. *The Red Hot Vacuum.* New York: Atheneum, 1970, pp. 148-149, 254-255.

> Styron is included in a long list of "younger American writers" who specialize in showing the baser elements of human character.

81. Spiller, Robert E. *et. al. Literary History of the United States.* 3rd ed. rev. New York: The Macmillan Company, 1963.

    Briefly describes Styron as an "existential" writer, owing to the recent publication of *Set This House on Fire.*

82. Spiller, Robert E. *A Time of Harvest: American Literature 1910-1960.* New York: Hill and Wang, 1962, pp. 147-148.

    Styron deals with intensive intrigues, "with the formation and dissolution of relationships within a closed human network" in "his picture of the dark entanglements of society in the American South" in *Lie Down in Darkness.* Criticism is limited to this single work by Styron.

83. Starke, Catherine Juanita. *Black Portraiture in American Fiction: Stock Characters, Archetypes, and Individuals.* New York: Basic Books, Inc., Publishers, 1971, pp. 120, 123, 214-215.

    Styron's portrait of Nat Turner reduces "a black culture-hero to a pathetically fallible creature, though one not totally stripped of admirable characteristics." An unexpectedly brief treatment of Styron's Nat Turner.

84. Stevenson, David L. "Novelists of Distinction." *The Creative Present.* Eds. Norma Balakian and Charles Simons. New York: Doubleday, 1963, pp. 195-212.

    Traces the European influence of Styron, Bellow, and others.

85. Straumann, Heinrich. *American Literature in the Twentieth Century.* 3rd ed. rev. New York: Harper & Row, 1965, p. 98.

    Calls *Lie Down in Darkness* a "well-balanced story about the general deterioration of a lawyer's family in Virginia as a result of character failings." Briefly summarizes the novel.

86. Stuckey, W.J. *The Pulitzer Prize Novels: A Critical Back-*

ward Look. Norman, Oklahoma: University of Oklahoma Press, 1966, pp. 157-158.

Styron's *Lie Down in Darkness* was a respectable candidate for the 1952 Pulitzer Prize.

87. Sullivan, Walter. *A Requiem for the Renaissance: The State of Fiction in the Modern South.* Athens: University of Georgia Press, 1976.

Styron "has all the equipment that a first-rate novelist needs, and he may even be a man of genius, but out of the pressures of our time and whatever perversities work within him, he has wasted himself on the doctrines of existentialism and on his celebrated thrust into the black past." Sullivan, a noted critic, writes convincingly, albeit with a tendency to generalize.

88. Sullivan, Walter. "The New Faustus." *Southern Fiction Today: Renascence and Beyond.* Ed. George Core. Athens: University of Georgia Press, 1969.

Sullivan seeks to exonerate Styron from attacks by black critics, saying Styron's Nat is "a new creation, a man with a voice that is insistently modern and therefore insistently hopeless."

89. Sullivan, Walter. "The New Faustus." *Death by Melancholy: Essays on Modern Southern Fiction.* Baton Rouge: Louisiana State University Press, 1972, pp. 97-113.

Reprint from Core, *Southern Fiction Today.* See entry above.

90. Thelwell, Mike. "The White Nat Turner." *Americans from Africa.* Ed. Peter I. Rose. New York: Atherton Press, 1970.

One of the contributors to *Ten Black Writers Respond* issues another attack on Styron and his novel.

91. Thorp, Willard. *American Writing in the Twentieth Century.* Cambridge: Harvard University Press, 1960, p. 234.

Styron is included in a list of writers of "the general literary renaissance taking place in many sections of the country."

92. Tischler, Nancy M. *Black Masks: Negro Characters in Modern Southern Fiction.* University Park, Pennsylvania: The Pennsylvania State University Press, 1969, p. 193.

A surprisingly brief treatment of *The Confessions of Nat Turner.* Tischler says Styron avoids the two principal stereotypes of Negroes in fiction, the contented slave and the brute. Tischler's book will disappoint Styron scholars. Perhaps the controversy over the novel scared Tischler away from an in-depth examination.

93. Tragle, Henry I. *Southampton Slave Revolt of 1831: A Compilation of Source Material.* Amherst: University of Massachusetts Press, 1971.

An authoritative account of available source material of the actual insurrection. Tragle faults Styron for distorting history. This is an extra-literary source of little value other than for historians.

94. Tytell, John. *Naked Angels: The Lives and the Literature of the Beat Generation.* New York: McGraw-Hill Book Co., 1976.

Mentions Styron's sense of weariness upon realizing that World War II had stretched itself into the Cold War. Little amplification beyond this statement.

95. Urang, Gunnar. "The Voices of Tragedy in the Novels of William Styron." *Adversity and Grace: Studies in Recent American Literature.* Ed. Nathan A. Scott, Jr. Chicago: University of Chicago Press, 1968, pp. 183-209.

"Styron's novels are 'serious'; they confront us with real suffering and compel us to feel that anguish as our own. Styron thus commits himself to an old-fashioned enthusiasm about 'character' and 'story.' "

96. Walcutt, Charles Child. "Idea Marching on One Leg: William Styron's *The Long March.*" *Man's Changing Mask: Modes and Methods of Characterization in Fiction.* Minneapolis: University of Minnesota Press, 1966, pp. 251-256.

   "In his novelette *The Long March* (1952) William Styron has gathered all his forces to dramatize an idea about Jewish character. It is as unsympathetic as it is suggestive. It generates a great deal of imaginative power; and it seems to be going deep into the roots of character until its symbolic purpose takes open charge and reduces the action to an expository contrivance."

97. Watkins, Floyd C. *The Death of Art: Black and White in the Recent Southern Novel.* Athens: University of Georgia Press, 1970.

   Cass Kinsolving of *Set This House on Fire* cannot rid himself of guilt feelings over the Negro.

98. Watkins, Floyd C. *In Time and Place: Some Origins of American Fiction.* Athens: The University of Georgia Press, 1976.

   Watkins assesses the verity with which seven twentieth-century novelists portray their cultural and geographical roots. The writers are Styron, John Steinbeck, Willa Cather, Sinclair Lewis, William Faulkner, Scott Momaday, and Margaret Mitchell. Watkins belongs to a select group of critics who consistently write intelligently and authoritatively about Southern Fiction.

99. Weales, Gerald. *The Jumping-Off Place: American Drama in the 1960's.* Toronto: The Macmillan Company, 1969, p. 149.

   "In 'This Quiet Dust' (*Harper's*, April 1965) William Styron tried to clarify some of the attitudes toward the Negro with which he grew up in the South." The primary source deals with Styron's involvement with prison reform.

100. Weber, Olga D., ed. *Literary and Library Prizes.* 6th ed. rev. New York: Harcourt, Brace & World, Inc., 1956, p. 13.

> Cites Styron for having won the Prix de Rome of the American Academy of Arts and Letters for *Lie Down in Darkness.* A brief entry.

101. Weinberg, Helen. *The New Novel in America: The Kafkan Mode in Contemporary Fiction.* Ithaca: Cornell University Press, 1970, pp. x, xii, xv, xvii, 124, 186, 191, 192, 195.

> No comments on *The Confessions of Nat Turner* are included. Considerable attention is given to *Set This House on Fire* which Weinberg sees as having "love, beauty, grace (grace in the religious sense)."

102. West, James L.W. III. "William Styron." *Dictionary of Literary Biography,* Vol. II. Detroit: Gale Research Company, 1978.

> West provides an excellent biographical account of Styron's life. Contains material appearing in no other sources to date. A valuable and well-written article.

103. Witham, W. Tasker. *The Adolescent in The American Novel, 1920-1960.* New York: Frederick Ungar Publishing Co., 1964, pp. 58, 69, 248, 252, 265, 270.

> Peyton Loftis is one of many characters in novels from the forties and fifties who are adolescents with deep psychological problems depicted through symbolism. An illuminating view of the major character in *Lie Down in Darkness.*

104. Woodward, C. Vann. *"The Confessions of Nat Turner."* *The Critic as Artist: Essay on Books 1920-1970.* Ed. Gilbert A. Harrison. New York: Liveright Publishing Company, 1972.

> A historian defends Styron's right as a novelist to borrow from history for his fictional creations. Woodward, author of *The Strange Career of Jim Crow,* and other studies of the South, praises Styron's novel.

105. Wright, Nathalia. *American Novelists in Italy.* Philadelphia: University of Pennsylvania Press, 1965, p. 23.

> Styron's characters seem to be in search of something and often acquire in Italy a sense of direction or a feeling of human brotherhood. Italy is the principal setting for *Set This House on Fire.* No amplification.

CRITICAL ARTICLES

A special note on the critical articles dealing with *The Confessions of Nat Turner* is necessary here. Much of what pretends to pass for literary criticism concerning this novel is actually a socio-historical consideration having little, if anything, to do with an author's right to create characters and to imbue them with individual features. The controversy over whether Styron's novel is faithful or unfaithful to history has small bearing on its worth as fiction. Scholars should be forewarned that much of this type of criticism, now removed some distance from the tempestuous period of the late sixties when the book appeared, has an obfuscating sameness about it. Exceptions to this admittedly general statement occur in the annotations when appropriate.

1. Akin, E. William. "Toward an Impressionistic History: Pitfalls and Possibilities in William Styron's Meditation on History." *American Quarterly*, 21, iv (Winter 1969), 805-812.

> Styron's novel misses the mark because of the dangers of overlaying creative features on a historical event or character. This same charge is repeated with only slight variations in numerous critical articles.

2. Aldridge, John W. "Highbrow Authors and Middlebrow Books." *Playboy*, 11 (April 1964), 173-174.

   Styron's novels are "middlebrow" while trying to appear "highbrow." Considering the "low-brow" source of this article, scholars should be wary of Aldridge's assertions.

3. Anderson, Jervis. "Styron and His Black Critics." *Dissent*, 16 (March-April 1969), 157-166.

   Anderson disagrees with those critics who "demand that literature should serve the immediate ideological interests of the black community...," but feels that Styron should have shown "the need for moral change."

4. Aptheker, Herbert. "Styron-Turner and Nat Turner: Myth and Truth." *Political Affairs*, 46 (October 1967), 40-50.

   On *The Confessions of Nat Turner*, Aptheker says, "Whatever this book is, it certainly is not the slave society of 19th century Virginia, where Turner lived and whose foundations he shook, which are in this novel." Criticizes the novel for its historical inaccuracies and its perpetuation of racial setreotypes.

5. Aptheker, Herbert. "A Note on the History." *The Nation*, 16 October 1967, pp. 375-376.

   One of Styron's more vocal critics, historian Aptheker takes exception to historical inaccuracies in *The Confessions of Nat Turner*.

6. Aptheker, Herbert, and William Styron. "Truth and Nat Turner." *The Nation*, 22 April 1968, pp. 543-547.

   A written debate between the two writers over Styron's right to use historical sources for his novel. This exchange is occasionally bitter.

7. Arnavon, Cyrille. "Les romans de William Styron." *Europe*, 41 (September 1963), 54-66.

   A critical assessment of Styron's first three

novels. Styron's popularity in France results from this and similar views of his work. Focuses on Peter Leverett's attitude toward the millionaire Mason Flagg in *Set This House on Fire.*

8. Askin, Denise. "The Half-Loaf of Learning: A Religious Theme in *The Confessions of Nat Turner.*" *Christianity and Literature*, 21, iii (1972), 8-11.

Nat Turner's rebellion results from an unfortunate blend of education with religious fervor. Askin's thesis is well-taken. The Reverend Whitehead justifies through scripture the institution of slavery. Nat Turner uses religion to foment rebellion.

9. Asselineau, Roger. "En suivant *La marche de nuit* de William Styron." *La Revue des Lettres Modernes*, Nos. 157-171 (1967), 73-83.

The universality of Styron's *The Long March* lies in the idea that "human life is an interminable forced march in the night and the 'never-endingness of war,' like 'movie film pieced together by an idiot.' " Asselineau, a proponent of the *nouveau roman*, writes convincingly about Styron.

10. Barzelay, D. and R. Sussman. "William Styron on *The Confessions of Nat Turner.*" *Yale Literary Magazine*, 137 (September 1968), 24-35.

Styron, while not an alumnus of Yale, is a Fellow of Silliman College, Yale. This interview relates Styron's view of what he is trying to do in his novel. The interview is lively and informative.

11. Baudrillard, Jean. "La Proie des Flammes," *Les Temp Modernes*, 193 (June 1962), 1928-37.

"Above all Styron eliminates the theological or puritan hypothesis about evil: the slow elucidation of the murder reveals that we here no longer have an individual or racial fatality,

or a personal one, but a shared manner of con-
duct, and exchange of guilts, a responsibility
that has been lived through."

12. Baumbach, Jonathan. "Paradise Lost: The Novels of William
Styron," *South Atlantic Quarterly*, 63 (Spring 1964), 207-
217.

Reprinted in *The Landscape of Nightmare*.
Overview of Styron's first three novels. *Set
This House on Fire* is not as bad a most critics
have contended. Its weakness is its occasional
didacticism. Styron seems "unable to conceive
of a sensitive human being who could with-
stand the nightmare of existence without the
anesthetic of drink."

13. Behar, Jack. "History and Fiction." *Novel*, 3 (Spring 1970),
260-265.

Styron's *The Confessions of Nat Turner* shows
the author's creative process by imbuing Nat
with psychological overtones. "There is no
question for me of Styron's right to construct
a Nat Turner according to some institutions
about the intense and unresolvable psychological trouble of a black man caught up in a baff-
lingly highminded and murderously inhuman
slave system." One of the more "literary" treatments of the question of historicity.

14. Benson, Alice R. "Techniques in the Twentieth-Century Novel
for Relating the Particular to the Universal: *Set This House
on Fire.*" *Papers of the Michigan Academy of Science*,
47 (1962), 587-594.

Draws a parallel between Joyce's treatment of
the *Odyssey* in *Ulysses* and Styron's reworking
of *Oedipus at Colonnus* in *Set This House on
Fire*. Scholarly and demanding reading.

15. Bilotta, J.D. "Critique of Styron's *Confessions of Nat Turner.*"
Negro History Bulletin, 38 (December 1974), 326-327.

This article is a restatement of previous argu-

ments against Styron's novel. Shallow and un-
illuminating.

16. Boatwright, James. "Reflexions sur Styron, ses critiqⁿes
et ses sources." *La Revue des Lettres Modernes*, Nos.
157-61 (1967), 123-135.

Traces literary influences on Styron's first
three novels. These numbers of the *Revue* are
edited by Melvin Friedman and are bound as
one volume.

17. Bonnichon, Andre. "William Styron et le second Oedipe."
Etudes, 13 (October 1962), 94-103.

Cass Kinsolving of *Set This House on Fire*
stumbles into awareness after the fashion of
Oedipus Rex. This article demonstrates Styron's popularity in France.

18. Brandriff, Welles T. "The Role of Order and Disorder in *The
Long March.*" *English Journal*, 56 (January 1967), 54-59.

Captain Mannix fails in his attempt to establish
"order" in the "disorderly" system of the Marine Corps. He now understands the world in
which he must live and struggle.

19. Briere, Annie. "La Proie des Critiques." *Nouvelles Literaires*,
22 March 1962, p. 8.

An interview with Styron, Michel Butor and
Maurice-Edgar Coindreau. Butor wrote the
"Preface" to Coindreau's French translation
of *Set This House on Fire* (Gallimard, 1962).

20. Bryant, Jerry H. "The Hopeful Stoicism of William Styron."
South Atlantic Quarterly, 42 (Autumn 1963), 539-550.

Styron's theme is "What must man endure?"
Each of Styron's first three novels offers a different answer. Styron's novels "dramatize the
despair of lost innocence and the hope which
rises from the power to endure." Bryant's article, even without a consideration of *Nat Turn-*

er, represents a significant critical contribution.

21.   Bulgheroni, Marisa. "William Styron: Il romanziere, il tempo e la storia." *Studi Americani,* 16 (1970), 407.28.

22.   Butor, Michel. "Preface." *La Proie des Flammes.* Trans. M.-E. Coindreau. Paris: Gallimard, 1962.

This preface to the French translation of *Set This House on Fire* reinforces the idea that Styron writes in the mode of the *nouveau roman* (avant-garde fiction). Concentrates on the use of the Oedipus myth in understanding the character Cass Kinsolving.

23.   Cambon, Glauco. "Faulkner fa scoula." *La Fiera Letteraria,* 7 March 1954, p. 5.

Shows the Faulknerian influence on *Lie Down in Darkness.*

24.   Canzoneri, Robert, and Page Stegner. "An Interview with William Styron." *Per/Se,* 1 (Summer 1966), 37-44.

Recorded when Styron was working on *Nat Turner.* Styron discusses at length what he is trying to do in the novel. Discusses the sexual aspects of the relationship between Nat and Margaret Whitehead. A very important source.

25.   Carver, Wayne. "The Grand Inquisitor's Long March." *University of Denver Quarterly,* 1 (1966), 37-64.

"The rebellious Christ (Mannix)...is changed by his regard for human dignity into a Satan-Christ serving the ends of what he rebels against." Styron's Colonel Templeton resembles Dostoyevsky's the Grand Inquisitor.

26.   Chapsal, Madeleine. "Entretien." *L'Express,* 8 March 1962, pp. 26-27.

An interview with Styron on the occasion of his publication of *Set This House on Fire.* Sty-

ron says "Americans do not like to learn that
people can be unbalanced, desperate, sometimes corrupt, that life can be horrible."

27. Cheshire, Ardner R., Jr. "The Recollective Structure of
The Confessions of Nat Turner." *The Southern Review*,
12 (January 1976), 110-21.

The recollective character of the hero's meditation on past experience provides the structural key to the novel. Uses Gabriel Marcel's
The Mystery of Being (1950) as an aid to explication.

28. Cheyer, A.H. "W.L.B. Biography: William Styron." *Wilson
Library Bulletin*, 36 (April 1962), 691.

A biographical overview of Styron.

29. Cleland, James T. "Reflections on Nat Turner." A Sermon
preached in the Duke University Chapel, June 14, 1968.
(Printed copies available from the Duke University Library.)

Uses Styron's novel as a springboard for a
lesson on racism. This is a homiletical rather
than a literary approach to the book.

30. Cockshutt, Rod. "An Evening with Willie (Morris) and Bill
(Styron)." *Raleigh News and Observer*. 18 April 1971,
p. 6.

An informal account of "supper table conver-
sation" with Styron and Willie Morris, former
editor of *Harper's*.

31. Coles, Robert. "Backlash." *Partisan Review*, 35 (Winter 1968),
128-133.

William Styron's *Nat Turner* is a powerful and
truthful book, one that captures the "thing"
that goes on between blacks and southern
whites. Styron "succeeds in making Nat a particular human being and a particular Negro."

32. Cooke, Michael. "Nat Turner's Revolt." *Yale Review*, 57 (Winter 1968), 273-278.

> "William Styron, in *The Confessions of Nat Turner*, rivals (Ralph) Ellison in imaginative candor, in the independence of mind and of temper that suggests original views."

33. Cooke, Michael. "Nat Turner: Another Response." *Yale Review*, 58 (Winter 1969), 295-301.

> "From first to last *The Confessions of Nat Turner* reminds us that it is a world lacking in 'logic,' a world of 'madness, illusion, error, dream, strife.' " This article is a sequel to the entry above.

34. Core, George. *"The Confessions of Nat Turner* and the Burden of the Past." *Southern Literary Journal*, 2 (Spring 1970), 117-134.

> "In *The Confessions of Nat Turner* William Styron is primarily concerned about depicting his characters fictively, from within—against a setting which must be at once historical and contemporaneous." Core is a perceptive critic whose comments merit attention.

35. Core, George. *"Nat Turner* and the Final Reckoning of Things." *Southern Review*, 4 (Spring 1968), 745-751.

> *The Confessions of Nat Turner* "is saturated with the feeling of actuality: in it the author has a sure grasp of the concrete and the imagined whole: this involves a sense of locality, of particular place, as a dramatic dimension of the action; a sense of the interplay of past and present, and the way a dramatic moment can bind them together; and, finally, a tragic sense of life with its inescapable waste, violence, corruption, and evil."

36. Cowley, Malcolm. "American Novels Since the War." *New Republic*, 28 December 1953, pp. 16-18.

Cites *Lie Down in Darkness* as representing
"the most hopeful tendency now to be found in
American fiction" because it deals "with human
characters, involved in human dilemmas."

37. Cunliffe, Marcus. "Black Culture and White America." *Encounter*, 34 (January 1970), 22-35.

"Nearly all the white reviewers gave high
praise to Styron. He had written a 'liberal'
novel, depicting Nat Turner as a sensitive,
isolated man tormented by religious and sexual
fantasies; and clearly only a man in torment
would have staged so desperate a massacre.
If the novel had appeared ten years earlier,
Negro reviewers might have been equally cordial. But in the new climate of opinion black critics were infuriated."

38. Curtis, Bruce. "Fiction, Myth and History in William Styron's *Nat Turner.*" *University College Quarterly*, 16 (January 1971), 27-32.

Basically, this is an extrinsic approach, not an
intrinsic examination of the novel as fictional
creation.

39. Davis, Robert G. "Styron and the Students." *Critique*, 3 (Summer 1960), 37-46.

A teacher of writing tells how he and his students found *Set This House on Fire* uneven:
very well-written in places, but overwritten in
others. A good examination of Styron's prose
style.

40. Delaney, Lloyd T. "A Psychologist Looks at *The Confessions of Nat Turner.*" *Psychology Today*, 1 (January 1968), 11-14.

Turner seeks to destroy the father image which
at once frees him and keeps him in bondage.
A concise psychological overview of the novel.
This is a companion article to Platt, Gerald M.,
cited below.

41. De Saint Phalle, Therese. "William Styron: 'En U.R.S.S.—
     et en France—je suis chez moi.' " *Le Figaro Litteraire*,
     28 October 1968, p. 26.

     An interview with Styron on his return from
     a writer's conference in the Soviet Union. Sty-
     ron comments on his consistency of writing
     about downtrodden characters.

42. Doar, Harriet. "Interview with William Styron," *Red Clay
     Reader, 1964.* Charlotte, North Carolina: *Southern Re-
     view,* 1964.

     On the arts staff of *The Charlotte Observer,*
     Doar queries Styron about his North Carolina
     connections such as studying at Davidson and
     at Duke with William Blackburn.

43. Driver, Tom F. "Black Consciousness Through a White
     Scrim." *Motive,* 27 (February 1968), 56-58.

     Styron sees Turner's blackness as a white per-
     son because of the insurmountable barrier
     of race. Carried to its limits, Driver's view
     would prohibit a black writer from creating a
     white character.

44. Duberman, Martin. "Historical Fictions." *New York Times
     Book Review,* 11 August 1968, pp. 1, 16-17.

     A rebuttal to attacks on *The Confessions of
     Nat Turner.*

45. Durden, R.F. "William Styron and His Black Critics." *South
     Atlantic Quarterly,* 68 (Spring 1969), 181-187.

     A review of Clarke's *William Styron's The Con-
     fessions of Nat Turner.* See from this same
     issue Holder, Alan, listed below.

46. Eggenschwiler, D. "Tragedy and Melodrama in *The Confes-
     sions of Nat Turner." Twentieth Century Literature,* 20
     (January 1974), 19-33.

     A structural examination of the novel for its
     historical, sociological, religious, and psycho-

logical forms in an attempt to see how the book can engender "so many approaches and cause so much controversy." A good overview of the elements of the controversy.

47. Emmanuel, Pierre. "L'historie d'un solitaire." *Preuves*, 19 (April 1969), 17-20.

    "Enclosed within himself, Nat is one of God's elect because of his chastity, but his erotic fantasies with images of white women, symbols of purity, of inaccessibility, precipitate violence." Not available in English, Emmanuel's article is perceptive.

48. Fenton, Charles A. "William Styron and the Age of the Slob." *South Atlantic Quarterly*, 59 (Autumn 1960), 469-476.

    Set This House on Fire is an attempt by Styron to render the national mood in terms of powerful characters of fiction. Styron is a greatly gifted writer and succeeds in a driving effort.

49. Flanders, Jane. "William Styron's Southern Myth." *Louisiana Studies*, 15 (Fall 1976), 263-278.

    Traces the pattern of Styron's "Southernness" through his three novels. *The Long March* is excluded.

50. Forkner, Ben, and Gilbert Schricke. "An Interview with William Styron." *Southern Review*, 10 (Autumn 1974), 923-934.

    The authors, with Styron in France on a lecture tour, discuss Styron's forthcoming novel about a woman who survives a Nazi concentration camp. An excellent interview.

51. Foster, Richard. "An Orgy of Commerce: William Styron's *Set This House on Fire*," *Critique*, 3 (Summer 1960), 59-70.

    Special attention is given to the structure and characterization of *Set This House on Fire*. Styron uses a Conradian "discontinuous structuring" which involves "backward and forward time-shifts following the quest of the seeking conscience."

52. Franklin, Jimmie L. *"Nat Turner* and Black History." *Indian Journal of American Studies,* 1, iv (1971), 1-6.

Yet another tedious citing of historicity.

53. Friedman, Joseph. "Non-Conformity and the Writer." *Venture,* 20 (Winter 1957), 23-31.

54. Friedman, Melvin J. *"The Confessions of Nat Turner:* The Convergence of 'Nonfiction Novel' and 'Meditation of History.' " *Journal of Popular Culture,* 1 (Fall 1967), 166-175.

Reprinted in Friedman's *William Styron* (Bowling Green, Ohio: Bowling Green University Popular Press, 1974, pp. 11-18) "Despite the caution expressed by several reviewers there is no reason to doubt the value of the point of view and narrative mode used in *The Confessions of Nat Turner."* Friedman provides focus and reasoned thinking on Styron's novel.

55. Friedman, Melvin J. "William Styron: An Interim Appraisal." *English Journal,* 50 (March 1961), 149-158, 192.

Reprinted in *William Styron* (Bowling Green, Ohio: Bowling Green University Popular Press, 1974, pp. 1-11). An overview critical essay on Styron's first three novels. "Styron has been conscientiously listened to and been taken seriously both in and out of the university." *Set This House on Fire* shows the influence of the French Existential writers.

56. Friedman, Melvin J. "William Styron et le nouveau roman." *La Revue des Lettres Modernes,* Nos. 157-161 (1967), 85-109.

Reprinted in *William Styron* (Bowling Green, Ohio: Bowling Green University Popular Press, 1974, Chapter Two). Focuses on *Set This House on Fire* as an example of the avant-garde fiction popular in France, citing this as one reason for Styron's popularity in that country. "Styron

seems to be consciously offering a pastiche of
the earlier generation's obsession with time
and its symbols."

57. Galloway, David D. "The Absurd Man as Tragic Hero: The
    Novels of William Styron." *Texas Studies in Literature
    and Language*, 6 (Winter 1965), 512-534.

    Makes a favorable, extensive, convincing survey
    of Styron's three novels as following the themes
    of Camus. Reprinted in *The Absurd Hero in
    American Fiction: Updike, Styron, Bellow,
    Salinger.* Austin: University of Texas Press,
    1966.

58. Geismar, Maxwell. "The Contemporary American Short
    Story." *Studies on the Left*, 4 (Spring 1964), 21-27.

59. Geismar, Maxwell. "The Post-War Generation in Arts and
    Letters." *Saturday Review of Literature*, 14 March 1953,
    pp. 11-12, 60.

    Mentions Styron among writers who are likely
    to combine the points of view of expatriate and
    native realist. Calls Styron a "promising" young
    writer.

60. Genovese, Eugene. "Nat Turner's Black Critics." *New York
    Review of Books*, 12 September 1968, pp. 34-37.

    A rebuttal to attacks on *The Confessions of
    Nat Turner.* Genovese expresses the view that
    Styron, as novelist, properly deals with the
    character of Nat Turner.

61. Gilman, Richard. "Nat Turner Revisited." *New Republic*,
    27 April 1968, pp. 23-32.

    Essay review of *Nat Turner* that claims Sty-
    ron's inability to imagine what it was like to be
    black, not his historical inaccuracy, produces
    a mediocre novel.

62. Gross, Seymour L. and Bender, Eileen. "History and Politics
    and Literature: The Myth of Nat Turner." *American Quar-*

terly, 23 (October 1971), 486-518.

It is the intention of this essay "to show that (Nat Turner) belongs to all of us as he has always belonged to those who used him—as a myth, as an imagined configuration of convictions, dreams, hopes, and fears." Reprinted in Morris, *The Achievement of William Styron* (1975).

63. Halpern, Daniel. "Checking in with William Styron." *Esquire,* August 1972, pp. 143-143.

An interview at Styron's home in Roxbury. At the time of the interview Styron was working on *The Way of the Warrior,* an unfinished novel. Styron discusses his mistrust of black intellectuals as a result of the harsh criticism of *The Confessions of Nat Turner.*

64. Harnack, Curtis. "The Quiddities of Detail." *Kenyon Review,* 30 (Winter 1968), 125-32.

"Writing as (Styron) is today, with our bitingly explicit Negro writers—particularly LeRoi Jones, James Baldwin, and the late Malcolm X—he comes up modern fashion and puts Nat's explosion into a shape today's readers can appreciate and even believe in: the religious impulse is psychologically explained in terms of sex."

65. Hassan, Ihab. "The Novel of Outrage: A Minority Voice in Postwar American Fiction." *American Scholar,* 34 (Spring 1965), 239-253.

Groups Styron, Baldwin, and Ellison in expressing "outrage" with humanity.

66. Hays, Peter L. "The Nature of Rebellion in *The Long March,*" *Critique,* 8 (Winter 1965-66), 70-74.

Attempts to find religious and mythical implication in *The Long March.* See *The Limping Hero* (1971) by Hays.

67. Hazard, Eloise Perry. "Eight Fiction Finds." *Saturday Review of Literature*, 16 February 1952, p. 17.

   Compares Styron to other young writers.

68. Hazard, Eloise P. "William Styron." *Saturday Review of Literature*, 15 September 1951, p. 12.

   Interview with Styron.

69. Hiers, John T. "The Graveyard Epiphany in Modern Southern Fiction: Transcendence of Selfhood." *Southern Humanities Review*, 9 (1975), 389-403.

   A discussion of the theme of death in the works of Agee, O'Connor, Wolfe, Humphrey, Welty, and Styron. Hiers doctoral dissertation was "Traditional Death Customs in Modern Southern Fiction."

70. Hoffman, Frederick J. "La Therapeutique de neant: Les romans de William Styron." *La Revue des Lettres Modernes* Nos. 157-161 (1967), 33-56.

   Styron's existentialism is an effort to establish man's individuality in a world of conformity.

71. Holder, Alan. "Styron's Slave: *The Confessions of Nat Turner.*" *South Atlantic Quarterly*, 68 (Spring 1969), 167-180.

   Styron's novel fails both as history and literature. Holder wins admiration for avoiding the "either-or" trap by condemning Styron on both counts.

72. Holman, C. Hugh. *"Confessions of Nat Turner,"* 20th Century American Novel cassette tape series, no. 94. Deland, Florida: Everett/Edwards Inc., 1971.

   A tape which commends Styron for undertaking the formidable task of attempting to enter the black consciousness.

73. Jones, James and William Styron. "Two Writers Talk it Over." *Esquire*, July 1963, pp. 57-59.

Styron talks about his plans for *The Confessions of Nat Turner* which he was writing at that time.

74. Kazin, Alfred. "The Alone Generation." *Harper's*, 219 (October 1959), 127-131.

In a critical overview of novels published since World War II, Kazin contends that "social intelligence is now lacking to our novelists— except to those brilliant Southern writers, like William Styron and Flannery O'Connor, who can find the present meaningful because they find the past so."

75. Klotz, Marvin. "The Triumph Over Time: Narrative Form in William Faulkner and William Styron." *Mississippi Quarterly*, 17 (Winter 1963-64), 9-20.

A comparative study of the treatment of Time as a motif in the works of Faulkner and Styron.

76. Kostelanetz, Richard. "The Bad Criticism of this Age." *Minnesota Review*, 4 (Spring 1964), 389-414.

77. Kretzoi, Charlotte. "William Styron: Heritage and Conscience." *Hungarian Studies in English*, 5 (1975), 121-136.

Focuses on *Lie Down in Darkness* and examines the deterioration of the Loftis family and the guilt accompanying that dissolution.

78. Lawson, John Howard. "Styron: Darkness and Fire in the Modern Novel." *Mainstream*, 13 (October 1960), 9-18.

Commenting on Peyton Loftis of *Lie Down in Darkness*, Lawson says, "The author knows, and we know, that the curse upon her is not nameless and that she is not alone; she is part of *us*, she is doomed by the waste and creativity and life that is the way of *our* world."

79. Lawson, Lewis. "Cass Kinsolving: Kierkegaardian Man of Despair." *Wisconsin Studies in Contemporary Literature*, 3 (Fall 1962), 54-66.

"Only when Cass Kinsolving, the protagonist, is viewed as a Kierkegaardian man of despair does his life take on enough significance to justify its very full presentation. For although he seems unaware of it, Kinsolving's descriptions of his thoughts and actions during his exile in Europe are couched in Kierkegaardian terms."

80. Lehan, Richard. "Existentialism in Recent American Fiction: The Demonic Quest." *Texas Studies in Language and Literature*, 1 (Summer 1959), 181-202.

    Mentions *Set This House on Fire* in the context of Existentialism.

81. Leon, Philip W. *"The Lost Boy* and a Lost Girl." *Southern Literary Journal,* 9 (Fall 1976), 61-69.

    Traces the influence of Thomas Wolfe's story on an early short story written while Styron was a student at Duke University. That story provided the starting point for *Lie Down in Darkness.*

82. Lewis, R.W.B. "American Letters: A Projection." *Yale Review,* 51 (December 1961), 211-226.

    "The names I make out for honor in the postwar generation include those of Ralph Ellison, Saul Bellow, James Purdy, William Styron, Norman Mailer, and J.D. Salinger."

83. Lewis, R.W.B. and C. Vann Woodward. "Slavery in the First Person: An Interview with William Styron." *Yale Alumni Magazine,* November 1967, pp. 37-39.

    One of the best of many interviews with Styron. Knowledgeable and provoking questions lead Styron into an excellent discussion of *The Confessions of Nat Turner.* Styron says, "There is no reason to draw strict parallels from Nat Turner in order to explicate current events. I would be appalled if some person tried to do this in a dogged and deterministic fashion. I did not intend that in the slightest."

84. Lichtenstein, G. "The Exiles." *New Statesman and Nation,* 6 September 1958, pp. 320-322.

   Discusses Styron as a member of the *Paris Review* group. Styron was one of the founders of the periodical.

85. Mailer, Norman. "Norman Mailer vs. Nine Writers." *Esquire,* 60 (July 1963), 63-69.

   Mailer takes on several writers, including Styron, and accuses him of "oiling the literary levers" to publish his books.

86. Markos, Donald W. "Margaret Whitehead in *The Confessions of Nat Turner.*" *Studies in the Novel,* 4 (Spring 1974), 52-59.

   Sexual frustration is "the underlying source of motivation for Nat Turner's uprising....Nat revolted to assert his manhood and his full dignity as a man." Margaret Whitehead, a white teenager, is the only victim of Nat Turner's slave uprising to die by Nat's hands.

87. Matthiessen, Peter and George Plimpton. "The Art of Fiction." *Paris Review,* 2 (Spring 1954), 42-57.

   An early interview with Styron's co-founders of the *Paris Review.* Styron eschews the "southern" label and comments on *Lie Down in Darkness.* Styron says he owes as much influence to Joyce and Flaubert as to Faulkner.

88. McNamara, Eugene. "William Styron's *Long March:* Absurdity and Authority." *Western Humanities Review,* 15 (Spring 1961), 267-272.

   The first critical examination of *The Long March.* Sees Mannix as Old Adam, (possibly Satan), Templeton as "priest," Culver as convert.

89. McNamara, Eugene. "The Post-Modern Novel." *Queen's Quarterly,* 69 (Summer 1961), 268-270.

Emphasis is placed on Styron in this broad
discussion of contemporary fiction.

90. Mellard, J.M. "Racism, Formula, and Popular Fiction."
     Journal of Popular Culture, 5 (Summer 1971), 10-37.

     "Like Baldwin, Williams, Jones, and others,
     (Styron) *interiorizes* the role of black-white
     sexual fantasies in the characterization of Nat
     Turner." Nat's fantasy rape develops his con-
     science and his consciousness.

91. Mellen, Joan. "Polemics: William Styron: The Absence of
     Social Definition." *Novel*, 4 (Winter 1971), 159-170.

     Accuses Styron of having a "dissembling atti-
     tude toward social and historical" dimensions
     of his subjects.

92. Moore, L. Hugh. "Robert Penn Warren, William Styron, and
     the Use of Greek Myth." *Critique*, 8 (Winter 1965-1966),
     75-87.

     Contends that Warren's *Wilderness* uses "My-
     thic elements (that) are more than imposed con-
     trivances," which is not the case with *Set This
     House on Fire*.

93. Morse, J. Mitchell. "Social Relevance, Literary Judgment,
     and the New Right; or, The Inadvertent Confessions of
     William Styron." *College English*, 30 (May 1969), 605-616.

     Reprinted in Morse, *The Irrelevant English
     Teacher*. Philadelphia: Temple University
     Press, 1972. An extremely harsh indictment of
     The Confessions of Nat Turner. Mitchell says
     the book "as a work of art doesn't exist."

94. Mudrick, Marvin. "Mailer and Styron: Guests of the Estab-
     lishment." *Hudson Review*, 17 (Autumn 1964), 346-366.

     The novels of Styron and Mailer have steadily
     degenerated, for each has "shown an inclination
     to sink his talents into journalism and literary
     politics, each apparently bent on retiring...
     into public life."

95. Nigro, August. *"The Long March:* The Expansive Hero in a Closed World." *Critique,* 9 (Winter 1967), 103-112.

   Captain Mannix rebels against his bondage, asserts his right to freedom but "the pride and will that move him to rebellion are also the tragic flaws that bind him to his own tyranny." Nigro sees Mannix in the tradition of Old Ben of Faulkner's "The Bear," as Ahab of *Moby Dick,* as Christ, Achilles, Atlas, Prometheus, Satan, Moses.

96. Nolte, William H. "Styron's Meditation on Saviors." *Southwest Review,* 58 (Autumn 1973), 338-348.

   "In place of Styron's highly strung and neurosis-driven savior, his critics would have us believe Nat was a heaven-kissing hero, half Julius Caesar and half Saint Francis of Assisi."

97. Normand, J. " 'Un Lit de Tenebre' de W. Styron: Variations sur le Theme de Tristan." *Etudes Americains,* 27 (January-March 1974), 64-71.

   Lie Down in Darkness derives from the medieval love-romance. Traces, as the title suggests, the tradition from Tristan to its manifestations in Styron's first novel.

98. Oates, S.B. "Styron and the Blacks—Another View." *Nation,* 31 May 1975, pp. 662-664.

99. O'Connell, Shaun. "Expense of Spirit: The Vision of William Styron." *Critique,* 8 (Winter 1965-1966), 20-33.

   Views Styron's first three novels as a continuum, "an increasingly complex vision of men detached from their old structural values of God, family, country, desperately seeking to infuse their lives with meaning."

100. Ownbey, Ray. "Discussions with William Styron," *Mississippi Quarterly,* 30 (Spring 1977), 283-295.

   Styron discusses his inability to finish a novel about the Marine Corps because of the intrusion

into his consciousness of the Vietnam War.
Also discusses the possibility of a television
movie based on *The Confessions of Nat Turner.*

101. Perry, J. Douglas, Jr. "Gothic as Vortex: The Form of Horror
in Capote, Faulkner, and Styron." *Modern Fiction Studies,*
19 (1973), 153-167.

"An examination of Capote, Faulkner, and Styron reveals that modern American gothic is not
only a matter of theme on image,....but of narrative form as well."

102. Platt, Gerald M. "A Sociologist Looks at *The Confessions
of Nat Turner.*" *Psychology Today,* 1 (January 1968), 14-15.

"The liberal masters who understood the slave's
plight and sympathized with him are guilty of
the most heinous crime of all—that of understanding and doing nothing." Examines the
characterization of Nat as a "marginal man"
caught between the black culture and the white.

103. Ratner, Marc L. "Rebellion of Wrath and Laughter: Styron's
Set This House on Fire." *Southern Review,* 7 (Autumn
1971), 1007-1020.

Styron's novel is satire, not tragedy. Styron
uses cartoon characters, caricatures, grotesques, bombast, and burlesque to achieve the
satiric effect.

104. Ratner, Marc L. "The Rebel Purged: Styron's *The Long
March.*" *Arlington Quarterly,* 2 (Autumn 1969), 27-42.

The Long March is a novel of rebellion that
culminates in *The Confessions of Nat Turner.*
All of Ratner's writings about Styron deal with
the theme of rebellion.

105. Ratner, Marc L. "Styron's Rebel." *American Quarterly,* 21
(Fall 1969), 595-608.

Writers who have attacked Styron's novel
"have completely ignored Styron's themes and
techniques in his earlier fiction in relation to

The Confessions of Nat Turner. Whether an article is written from a sociological or a literary point of view it is relevant that the critic examine the other works of a novelist before passing judgment on his current work."

106. Robb, Kenneth A. "William Styron's Don Juan." *Critique,* 8 (Winter 1965-1966), 34-46.

Contends that Styron's "use of the Don Juan legend via Mozart via Kierkegaard informs *Set This House on Fire* with a coherence and unity that correlates well with his depiction of Cass Kinsolving as a 'Kierkegaardian man of despair.' " Not for the novice reader, Robb's article is a primer on existentialism.

107. Rubin, Louis D. Jr. "The South and the Faraway Country." *Virginia Quarterly Review,* 38 (Summer 1962), 444-459.

An overview of recent Southern fiction. "The city began to seem merely big and ugly. The novels of the modern Southern writers contain numerous descriptions of young Southerners adrift in the metropolis (including) Peyton Loftis of *Lie Down in Darkness.*"

108. Rubin, Louis D., Jr. "William Styron and Human Bondage: *The Confessions of Nat Turner.*" *Hollins Critic,* 4 (December 1967), 1-12.

"A Negro seen by William Styron is in no important or essential way different from a white man. Social conditions, not heredity and biology, set him apart."

109. Rubin, Louis D., Jr. "William Styron and Human Bondage: *The Confessions of Nat Turner.*" *The Sounder Few,* ed. R.H.W. Dillard. Athens: University of Georgia Press, 1971.

Reprints Rubin's article from the *Hollins Critic.*

110. Rubin, Louis D., Jr. "An Artist in Bonds." *Sewanee Review,* 69 (Winter 1961), 174-179.

Set This House on Fire is a better novel than

Lie Down in Darkness and "deserves the respectful attention of anyone seriously interested in fiction—this despite a grievous structural flaw which in the hands of a less gifted author might have sufficed to spoil it entirely." Rubin is perhaps too kind in his remarks about *Set This House on Fire.*

111. Rubin, Louis D., Jr. "Notes on the Literary Scene: Their Own Language." *Harper's*, 230 (April 1965), 173-175.

Styron's *Lie Down in Darkness* is examined to show how Southern novelists differ from their older contemporaries such as Faulkner, Warren, and Porter.

112. Saloman, Michel. "Interview avec William Styron." *Magazine Literaire*, no. 27 (March 1969), 24-25.

113. Saradhi, K.P. "The Agony of a Slave Negro: Theme and Technique in Styron's *Nat Turner.*" *Osmania Journal of English Studies*, 9, i (1972), 11-19.

114. Schlesinger, Arthur, Jr. "Nationalism and History," speech delivered to the Association for the Study of Negro Life and History. 53rd Annual Meeting. (Housed with the Styron collection at Duke University.)

This noted historian defends Styron's artistic right to re-create Nat Turner: "Mr. Styron's aim was the imaginative depiction of Nat Turner as a human being."

115. Shapiro, Herbert. *"The Confessions of Nat Turner:* William Styron and His Critics." *Negro American Literature Forum*, 9 (1975), 99-104.

Styron proceeds from a pre-conceived view of the slave influenced by Stanley Elkins' thesis that slave personalities conformed to the "Sambo" stereotype.

116. Sink, D.M. "A Response to Critics: *The Confessions of Nat Turner.*" *Clearing House*, 48 (October 1973), 125-126.

117.   Stevenson, David L. "Styron and the Fiction of the Fifties."
       Critique, 3 (Summer 1960), 47-58.

       Discusses the major themes in Styron's fiction.
       Compares Styron's generation to the Lost Gen-
       eration. Peyton Loftis of *Lie Down in Darkness*
       is "the victim of the driving moral disorienta-
       tion of the generation which came to maturity
       after World War II."

118.   Sullivan, Walter. "The Decline of Regionalism in Southern
       Fiction." *Georgia Review*, 18 (Fall 1964), 300-308.

       "Between (James) Jones and Styron, Styron
       seems more polished, more sophisticated, more
       wise in the mores of the broad world. But as a
       writer, he exists in a kind of limbo, cut off
       from his tradition and unable to find any other,
       obligated to return home occasionally, but
       ignorant as to what such return might signi-
       fy."

119.   Suter, Anthony. "Transcendence and Failure: William Sty-
       ron's *Lie Down in Darkness.*" *Caliban XII* (Toulouse), 11
       (1975), 157-166.

       Discusses the suicide of Peyton Loftis as "the
       only act of hope" in *Lie Down in Darkness*.
       The other characters in the novel are unable
       to escape their self-imprisonment.

120.   Talese, Gay. "Looking for Hemingway." *Esquire*, July 1963,
       pp. 44-47, 106-110.

       An account of *"The Paris Review* crowd" who
       had gathered in George Plimpton's New York
       apartment for a party. Jacqueline Kennedy
       (then the First Lady) engages Styron in con-
       versation. Styron's caricature appears on page
       47 along with other members of Styron's lit-
       erary set.

121.   Thelwell, Mike. "Arguments: The Turner Thesis." *Partisan
       Review*, 35 (Summer 1968), 403-412.

A black writer attacks Styron's perpetuation of racial myths in Nat Turner. Turner's rebellion "is a consequence of the inevitable frustration" of despising his blackness and aspiring to whiteness.

122. Thelwell, Mike. "Mr. William Styron and the Reverend Turn.er." *Massachusetts Review*, 9 (Winter 1968), 7-29.

> Reprinted in J.H. Clarke, ed. *William Styron's The Confessions of Nat Turner: Ten Black Writers Respond.* Boston: Beacon, 1968, pp. 79-91.
> "William Styron's *The Confessions of Nat Turner* straddles two genres, claims to be not quite either, and manages to combine the problems of both while to an extent reaping dual dividends as a novel which is in some way also 'history.' "

123. Thorp, Willard. "The Southern Mode." *South Atlantic Quarterly*, 63 (Autumn 1964), 576-582.

> A review of Louis D. Rubin's *The Faraway Country: Writers of the Modern South* and John M. Bradbury's *Renaissance in the South: A Critical History of the Literature 1920-1960.* Rubin thinks Styron's *Set This House on Fire* is "an examination conducted on Southern terms," but Styron has given no indication that he "had written it in a new Southern mode."

124. Tischler, Nancy M. "Negro Literature and Classic Form." *Contemporary Literature*, 10 (Summer 1969), 352-365.

> Tischler cites Styron's *Nat Turner* and Ellison's *Invisible Man* as works of "great aesthetic value" for critical consideration. These authors do not present the stereotyped Negro character. See Vogler, T.A. "Reply to Nancy Tischler," cited below.

125. Tragle, Henry I. "Styron and His Sources." *Massachusetts Review*, 11 (Winter 1970), 134-153.

Tragle, author of the extensive compilation of source material *Southampton Slave Revolt of 1831* (Amherst, Massachusetts: University of Massachusetts Press, 1971), presents facsimiles of historical documents which Styron overlooked or ignored in his research for *The Confessions of Nat Turner.* Interesting as history but not as literary criticism.

126. Urang, Gunnar. "The Broader Vision: William Styron's *Set This House on Fire.*" *Critique,* 8 (Winter 1965-1966), 47-69.

An analysis of *Set This House on Fire* in terms of its ambitions, its achievements, and its failures: "Several critics have accused Styron of not having been ruthless enough about his material, of including much which he should have rejected. I find him vulnerable to this charge."

127. Vanderbilt, Kermit. "Writers of the Troubled Sixties." *Nation,* 17 December 1973, pp. 661-665.

"Six years after *(The Confessions of Nat Turner)* survived the attack of angry black writers and intellectuals who, understandably enough, assailed Styron's 'white liberal' distortion of Nat Turner as a black Hamlet, one can assess Styron's imaginative recasting of black history as the foremost literary event of 1967. No other writer who responded to the new black awareness of the period was to achieve Styron's historical range and his unsettling literary power."

128. Via, Dan O., Jr. "Law and Grace in Styron's *Set This House On Fire.*" *Journal of Religion,* 51 (April 1971), 125-136.

Attributes "the new appreciation" of *Set This House on Fire* to "a recognition of its theological significance." Cass Kinsolving achieves Christian grace. Via's article is perceptive and well-written.

129. Vogler, T.A. "Reply to Nancy Tischler." *Contemporary Liter-ature*, 11 (Winter 1970), 130-135.

Vogler contends that Nancy Tischler's treatment of Styron's Nat Turner is superficial.
He berates Tischler's "smooth" interpretation
of Styron's novel and of Ellison's *Invisible
Man.* See Tischler, Nancy M. "Negro Literature
and Classic Form," cited above.

130. West, James L.W. "William Styron's Afterword to *The Long
March.*" *Mississippi Quarterly*, 28 (Spring 1975), 185-186.

The first publication of the "Afterword" to the
Norwegian edition housed with Styron's papers
at The Library of Congress.

131. Williams, Ernest P. "William Styron and His Ten Black Critics: A Belated Meditation." *Phylon*, 37 (June 1976),
189-195.

Critics who accuse Styron of taking liberties
with history in *The Confessions of Nat Turner*
are guilty of distortions themselves by denying
Styron his rights as an author. A reflection
upon *William Styron's Nat Turner: Ten Black
Critics Respond* (1968).

132. Winner, Arthur. "Adjustment, Tragic Humanism and Italy."
Studi Americani, 7 (1961), 311-361.

A detailed discussion of *Set This House on
Fire.* Discusses the Italian setting as part of
Styron's desire to write a "gothic" moral tale
showing American concepts of innocence and
evil.

133. Woodward, C. Vann. "Confessions of a Rebel: 1831." *New
Republic*, 157 (October 1967), 27.

"Whatever accounts for Nat's rebellion, it was
not the irrepressible rage of the intolerably
oppressed." Woodward, a historian, does not
disparage Styron for his use of history as a
basis for fiction.

REVIEWS OF STYRON'S BOOKS

LIE DOWN IN DARKNESS

1. A.S. *Canadian Forum*, 21 (January 1952), 239.

2. Aldridge, John W. *New York Times Book Review*, 9 September 1951, p. 5.

3. Bedell, W.D. "William Styron—Bitter Story Hits Home," *Houston Post*, September 9, 1951, Sec. 1, p.22

4. Breit, Harvey. *Atlantic Monthly*, 188 (October 1951), 78-80.

5. Byam, M.S. *Library Journal*, 15 September 1951, pp. 1423-1424.

6. Chapin, Ruth. *Christian Science Monitor*, 4 October 1951, p. 11.

7. Cowley, Malcolm. *New Republic*, 125 (October 8, 1951), 19-20.

8. Crume, Paul. "Strong Novel of Virginia Tragedy," *Dallas Morning News*, 9 September 1951, Part VI, p. 7.

9. Davis, Robert G. *American Scholar*, 21 (Winter 1951-1952), 114, 116.

10. Davis, Robert G. "In a Ravelled World Love Endures." *New York Times Book Review*, 26 December 1954, pp. 1, 13.

11. Dempsey, David. "Talk with William Styron," *New York Times Book Review*, 9 September 1951, p. 27.

12. Derleth, August. *Chicago Sunday Tribune Magazine of Books*, 9 September 1951, p. 3.

13. Downing, Francis. *Commonweal*, 54 (October 5, 1951), 620.

14. Elwood, Irene. "Family Has Everything, Loses All," *Los Angeles Times*, 16 September 1951, Part IV, p. 5.

15. Geismar, Maxwell. *Saturday Review of Literature*, 15 September 1951, pp. 12-13.

16. Govan, Christine Noble. "Story of Weak Family is Plea for More Maturity in Adults," *Chattanooga Times*, 16 September 1951, p. 19.

17. Grove, Lee. "Memorable First Novel Demolishes a Family," *Washington (D.C.) Post*, 9 September 1951, p. 6B.

18. Hazard, Eloise P. "William Styron." *Saturday Review of Literature*, 15 September 1951, p. 12.

19. Hazard, Eloise P. *Saturday Review of Literature*, 16 February 1952, p. 17.

20. Heth, Edward Harris. "A Torrential New Talent," *Milwaukee Journal*, 16 September 1951, Sec. V, p. 5.

21. Hutchens, John K. "William Styron." *New York Herald Tribune Book Review*, 9 September 1951, p. 2.

22. Janeway, Elizabeth. *New Leader*, 21 January 1952, p. 25.

23. Jones, Carter Brooke. "Work of Virginia's William Styron Hailed as Extraordinary 1st Novel," *Washington (D.C.) Sunday Star*, 9 September 1951, p. C-3.

24. Jones, Howard Mumford. *New York Herald Tribune Book Review*, 9 September 1951, p. 3.

25. Kelley, James E. "Promising First Novel—Violence of Love and Hate," *Denver Post,* 9 September 1951, p. 6E.

26. Kirby, John Pendy. *Virginia Quarterly Review,* 28 (Winter 1952), 129-130.

27. L(aycock), E(dward) A. "An Exciting Discovery—William Styron Writes Magnificent First Novel About a Tragic Family," *Boston Sunday Globe,* 9 September 1951, p. A-27.

28. Lambert, J.W. *London Sunday Times,* 30 March 1952, p. 3.

29. Mason, Robert. "Story of the Spirit is Rich in Poetry and Insight—William Styron of Newport News, 26, Is Suddenly a Major Novelist," *Norfolk, Virginian-Pilot,* 9 September 1951, Part 5, p. 4.

30. Munn, L.S. *Springfield Republican,* 30 September 1951, p. 10B.

31. *Newsweek,* 10 September 1951, pp. 106-107.

32. *The New Yorker,* 29 September 1951, pp. 118-119.

33. O'Brien, Alfred, Jr. *Commonweal,* 55 (October 9, 1951), 43-44.

34. O'Leary, Theodore M. "Styron's Remarkable First Novel," *Kansas City (Mo.) Star,* 29 September 1951, p. 16.

35. Pasley, Gertrude. "Unhappy People," *Newark (N.J.) Sunday News,* 16 September 1951, Sec. IV, p. 88.

36. Prescott, Orville. *The New York Times,* 10 September 1951, p. 19.

37. Ragan, Marjorie. "A New Southern Author Shows Literary Promise," *Raleigh (N.C.) News and Observer,* 16 September 1951, Sec. IV, p. 5.

38. Rubin, Louis D. *Hopkins Review,* 5 (Fall 1951), 65-68.

39. Scott, Eleanor M. *Providence (R.I.) Sunday Journal,* 9 September 1951, Sec. VI, p. 8.

40. Scott, J.D. *New Statesman and Nation*, 19 April 1952, p. 473.

41. Sessler, Betty. *Richmond (Va.) Times-Dispatch*, 16 September 1951, p. 8-A.

42. Sherman, John K. "First Novel Stamps Young Writer as Great," *Minneapolis (Minn.) Sunday Tribune*, 30 September 1951, Feature-News Section, p. 6.

43. Smith, Harrison. "Young Writer Depicts Trials of Human Soul," *Buffalo (N.Y.) Evening News*, 8 September 1951, Magazine Section, p. 7. See also *Charlotte (N.C.) Observer*, 9 September 1951, p. 14D; *Philadelphia Sunday Bulletin*, 9 September 1951, Magazine Sec., p. 6.

44. Snyder, Marjorie B. "Love, Hate, Passion All in His Book," *Boston Sunday Herald*, 9 September 1951, Sec. I, p. 6.

45. Stix, Frederick W. *Cincinnati Enquirer*, 9 September 1951, Sec. 3, p. 13.

46. Swados, Harvey. *Nation*, 24 November 1951, p. 453.

47. *Time*, 10 September 1951, p. 106.

48. Wallace, M. *Independent Woman*, 30 (November 1951), 325.

49. Ziegner, Edward. "Here's a First, Not a Last, We Hope." *Indianapolis (Ind.) News*, 8 September 1951, p. 2.

THE LONG MARCH

1. Boruel, Bernard. *Forces Nouvelles*, 13 June 1963, p. 13.

2. Bryden, Ronald. *Spectator*, 6 April 1962, p. 454.

3. de Ricaumont, Jacques. *Combat*, 18 July 1963, p. 9.

4. Haedens, Kleber. *Paris-Presse-L'Intrasigeant*, 15 June 1963, p. 15.

5. Hughes, Marion. *The Nation*, 7 June 1963, p. 5.

6. *Library Journal*, 15 June 1968, p. 2522.

7. Marx, Leo. *New Republic*, 31 October 1955, pp. 19-20.

8. Mohrt, Michel. *Nouveau Candide*, 16-23 May 1963, p. 16.

9. Philippon, Henri. *Aux Ecoutes*, 7 June 1963, p. 39.

10. *Punch*, 5 May 1962, p. 735.

11. Scannell, Vernon. *The Listener*, 19 April 1962, p. 701.

12. *Times Literary Supplement* (London), 6 April 1952, p. 229.

13. *Times Weekly Review*, 12 April 1962, p. 10.

14. Villelaur, Anne. *Lettres Francaises*, 18 July 1963, p. 2.

15. Zane, Maitland. *Time and Tide*, 12 April 1962, p. 30.

SET THIS HOUSE ON FIRE

1. Adams, Phoebe. *Atlantic Montly*, 206 (July 1960), 97-98.

2. A.M. *Nouveau Candide*, 1-9 March 1962, p. 17.

3. Baro, Gene. *New York Herald Tribune Book Review*, 5 June 1960, pp. 1, 12.

4. Betts, Doris. "Serious Violent Novel," *Houston Post*, 12 June 1960, Houston Now Section, p. 36.

5. Borklund, Elmer. *Commentary*, 30 (November 1960), 452-454.

6. Bourg, Gene. "Italy Is Scene of American Drama," *New Orleans Times-Picayune*, 19 June 1960, Sec. II, p. 3.

7. Bradley, Van Allen. "Second Styron Novel Close to a Masterpiece," *Chicago Daily News*, 4 June 1960, p. 13.

8. Breit, Harvey. *Partisan Review*, 28 (Summer 1960), 561-563.

9. Bryden, Ronald. *Spectator*, 17 February 1961, pp. 232-233.

10. C., M. *Carrefour*, 21 March 1962, p. 21.

11. Cabau, Jacques. *L'Express*, 22 February 1962, p. 33.

12. Cambon, Glauco. *Fiera Letteraria*, 22 November 1960, p. 4.

13. Castelnau, Marie-Pieree. *L'Information*, 17 March 1962, p. 11.

14. Cheney, Frances Neel, "Rich, Sensitive Prose—Eye for Detail," *Nashville (Tenn.) Banner*, 3 June 1960, p. 24.

15. Coindreau, Maurice-Edgar. *Nouveau Candide*, 15-22 March 1962, p. 17.

16. Covici, Pascal, Jr. "Powerful Vision for Our Time," *Dallas Morning News*, 5 June 1960, Sec. V., p. 6.

17. Creed, Howard. "Styron Doesn't Set Reviewer on Fire," *Birmingham (Ala.) News*, 21 August, 1960, Sec. E, p. 8.

18. Culligan, Glendy. "Styron Returns—Jury Still Hung," *Washington (D.C.) Post*, 5 June 1960, Sec. E, p. 6.

19. Cunningham, Bill. *San Antonio Express and News*, 10 July 1960, Sec. G, p. 5.

20. Curley, Thomas F. *American Scholar*, 29 (Autumn 1960), 552-560.

21. Dahms, Joseph. *America*, 18 June 1960, pp. 380-381.

22. Daniels, N.A. "The Identity of Opposites," *San Francisco People's World*, 9 July 1960, p. 6.

23. David, Jean. *Democratie*, 15 March 1962, p. 18.

24. Dawkins, Cecil. "Our Man in Italy—A Study of Evil and Its Expiation," *Milwaukee Journal*, 5 June 1960, Sec. 5,, p. 4.

25. De Saint-Phalle, Therese. *Revue de Paris*, 1 April 1962, p. 166.

26. Dumur, Guy. *France-Observateur*, 15 March 1963, p. 20.

27. Dwight, Ogden G. "In 'Set This House on Fire' Styron Has Quite a Blaze," *Des Moines (Iowa) Register*, 3 July 1960, Sec. G, p. 11.

28. Fuller, Edmund. *Chicago Sunday Tribune Magazine of Books*, 5 June 1960, p. 3.

29. Galey, Matthieu. *Arts, Lettres, Spectacles, Musique*. 14-20 March 1962, p. 4.

30. Galloway, David. *Night Watch*, I (May 1961), 20.

31. Gentry, Curt. *San Francisco Sunday Chronicle This World*, 5 June 1960, p. 22.

32. Gillespie, Annamarie. *Extension*, 55 (December 1960), 22.

33. Griffin, L.W. *Library Journal*, 15 June 1960, p. 2458.

34. Hayes, E. Nelson. "Novels by Styron and Fifield," *Providence (R.I.) Journal*, 5 June, 1960, Sec. W, p. 20.

35. Hicks, Granville, *Saturday Review of Literature*, 4 June 1960, p. 13.

36. Highet, Gilbert. *Book-of-the-Month-Club-News*. June 1960, p. 22.

37. Hill, Susan. *Time and Tide*, 24 February 1961, p. 285.

38. Hollander, John. *Yale Review*, 50 (September 1960), 152-153.

39. Hunter, Anna C. "Styron Fulfills Promise with Explosive New Novel," *Savannah (Ga.) Morning News*, 5 June 1960, Magazine, p. 14.

40. Hutchens, John. *New York Herald Tribune*, 3 June 1960, p. 11.

41. Jones, Carter B. "Mr. Styron's New Novel is a Disappointment," *Washington (D.C.) Sunday Star*, 5 June 1960, Sec. C, p. 11.

42. Kaufman, Clarence. "Second Styron Novel Proof of Major Talent," *Lincoln (Neb.) Sunday Journal and Star*, 5 June 1960, Sec. B, p. 12.

43. Kenney, Herbert Jr. "Moralizing Binge Spoils Styron Talent," *Indianapolis News*, 6 August 1960, p. 2.

44. *Kirkus*, 15 April 1960, p. 333.

45. Kirsch, Robert R. "Styron's 'House' Nears Greatness," *Los Angeles Times*, 5 June 1960, Sec. C, p. 7.

46. Kohn, Sherwood. "Styron...An Heir of Camus?" *Louisville (Ky.) Times*, 15 June 1960, p. 11.

47. L., E.A. "American Spoiled Boy—Styron's Third Novel Shocking, Powerful Picture of Degradation," *Boston Sunday Globe*, 5 June 1960, Sec. A., p. 7.

48. L., E.H. "New Book Plenty Hot—It Deserves to Burn," *Salt Lake Tribune*, 14 August 1960, Sec. W, p. 15.

49. La Rochefoucaulf, Marthe de. *Realites*, April 1962, p. 9.

50. Las Vergnas, Raymond. *Nouvelles Litteraires*, 29 March 1962, pp. 4-5.

51. Layton, Mike. "Critics Predictions Fulfilled by Styron," *Olympia (Wash.) Sunday Olympian*, 12 June 1960, p. 22.

52. Lea, George. "New Novel Won't Set House on Fire," *Chicago Sun-Times*, 10 July 1960, Sec. III, p. 5.

53 Lemaire, Marcel. *Revue des Langues Vivantes*, 28 (1962), 70-78.

54. "Life, Death of Sadistic Millionaire," *Miami Herald* 12 June 1960, Sec. J, p. 14.

55. Lindau, Betsy. *Asheville (N.C.) Citizen-Times*, 5 June 1960, Sec. D, p. 3.

56. Lowman, Ann. "Too Much Retrospect Mars Styron's Second," *Columbus (Ohio) Sunday Dispatch*, 26 June 1960, TAB Section, p. 12.

57. McDermott, Stephanie. "Arty People Flounder in Own Morass," *St Louis Globe Democrat*, 5 June 1960, Sec. F, p. 4.

58. McManis, John. *Detroit News*, 5 June 1960, Sec. F, p. 3.

59. Malcolm, Donald. *The New Yorker*, 4 June 1960, pp. 152-154.

60. Mason, Robert. "Characters Clash in Heroic Conflict," *Virginian Pilot and Portsmouth Star*, 5 June 1960, Sec. F, p. 8.

61. Michel, Marc. *Nouvelle Revue Francaise*, June 1962, pp. 1121-1123.

62. Miller, Nolan. *Antioch Review*. 20 (Summer 1960), 256.

63. Mizener, Arthur. *New York Times Book Review*, 5 June 1960, p. 5.

64. Monaghan, Charles. *Commonweal*, 22 July 1960, p. 380.

65. Mooney, Harry, Jr. "Styron Raises Issues, Faces Them Squarely, But Novel Is Seriously Marred by Author's Undisciplined Rhetoric," *Pittsburgh Press*, 5 June 1960, Sec. V, p. 14.

66. Murray, James G. *The Critic*, 19 (August-September 1960), 37.

67. Newberry, Mike. *Mainstream*, 13 (September 1960), 61-63.

68. *New Mexico Quarterly*, 301 (Winter 1960-1961), 412.

69. *Newsweek*, 6 June 1960, p. 117.

70. Nichols, Luther. "Styron's Literary Shock Treatment," *San Franciso Examiner*, 29 May 1960, Highlight Section, p. 6.

71. Nourissier, Francois. *Vogue*, May 1962, pp. 90-91.

72. O'Leary, Theodore M. "All the Elements of Greatness," *Kansas City (Mo.) Star*, 4 June 1960, p. 18.

73. Peckham, Stanton. "Styron's Second Novel Fulfills Promise," *Denver Sunday Post*, 5 June 1960, Roundup Section, p. 9.

74. Perkin, Robert L. "Important Fiction," *Rocky Mountain News*, (Denver), 26 June 1960, Sec. A, p. 14.

75. Pickrel, Paul. *Harper's*, 221 (July 1960), 93.

76. Prescott, Orville. *New York Times*, 3 June 1960, p. 29.

77. Price, Emerson. "Magnificent Novel Portrays Man Trapped by His Own Folly," *Cleveland Press*, 7 June 1960, p. 28.

78. Price, R.G. *Punch*, 15 March 1961, pp. 441-442.

79. Ragan, Marjorie. "A Brilliant Fire of Tragedy," *Raleigh (N.C.) News and Observer*, 5 June 1960, Sec. III, p. 5.

80. Rogers, W.G. "Killing in Italy Theme of New Styron Novel," *Cleveland Plain Dealer*, 12 June 1960, Sec. H, p. 8.

81. Rosenthal, Jean. *Informations et Documents*, 15 September 1961, p. 25.

82. Roth, Philip. *Commentary*, 31 (March 1961), 222-33.

83. Rothberg, Abraham. *New Leader*, 4-11 July, pp. 24-27.

84. Roy, Claude. *Liberation*, 20 March 1962, p. 7.

85. Rubin, Louis D., Jr. *Sewanee Review*, 64 (Winter 1961), 174-179.

86. Scott, Paul. *New Statesman and Nation,* 17 February 1961, pp. 270-271.

87. Sherman, John K. "Melodrama of Good and Evil Probes Human Undercurrents," *Minneapolis Tribune,* 12 June 1960, Sec. E, p. 6.

88. Sinclair, Reid B. "Prodigious Effort by a Virginian," *Richmond Times Dispatch,* 26 June 1960, Sec. L., p. 10.

89. Southern, Terry. *Nation,* 19 November 1960, p. 382.

90. *Time,* 6 June 1960, p. 98.

91. *Times Literary Supplement* (London), 17 February 1961 p. 101.

92. *Times Weekly Review,* 23 February 1961, p. 10.

93. Villelaur, Anne. *Les Lettres Francaises.* 8-14 March 1962, p. 2.

94. *Virginia Quarterly Review,* 36 (Autumn 1960), civ.

95. Watts, Harold H. "Assembly of Horrors," *St. Louis Post-Dispatch,* 19 June 1960, Sec. B, p. 4.

96. "William Styron Writes PW About His New Novel." *Publisher's Weekly,* 30 May 1960, pp. 4-5.

THE CONFESSIONS OF NAT TURNER

1. *America,* 25 November 1967, p. 666.

2. *America,* 24 February 1968, p. 269.

3. *American* (Chicago), 8 October 1967, Sec. III, p. 5.

4. Ancrum, Calhoun. "Novel by Styron Gets Rave Notices," *Charleston (W. Va.) News Courier,* 31 December 1967, Sec. D, p. 2.

5. Ayres, B. Drummond, Jr. "Negro Defends Uncle Tom as Powerful Character." *New York Times,* 25 February 1968, p. 58.

6. Barkham, John. "60 Whites Were Killed in 1831 Slave Riots," *Youngstown (Ohio) Vindicator,* 8 October 1967, Sec. B., p. 2. See also *Woodland (Cal.) Democrat,* 18 October 1967; *Lewiston (Idaho) Tribune,* 15 October 1967; *Albany (N.Y.) Times-Union,* 8 October 1967.

7. Bell, Bernard. *Michigan Quarterly Review,* 6 (Fall 1968), 282.

8. Bernstein, Victor. "Black Power, 1831," *Hadassah Magazine* (November 1967), 16, 37.

9. Billings, Claude. "Confessions Bares Negro Slave Revolt," *Indianapolis Star,* 17 December 1967, Sec. VIII, p. 7.

10. Birlchaui, John. "Nat Turner's Rampage Told," *Tucson (Ariz.) Daily Citizen,* 2 December 1967, Ole Magazine, p. 7.

11. *Booklist,* 1 December 1967, p. 425.

12. Bradley, Van Allen. "Styron Tells Slave's Saga," *Memphis Commercial Appeal,* 15 October 1967, Sec. V, p. 6. See also *Birmingham (Ala.) News,* 15 October 1967.

13. Braxton, P.N. *Book World,* 31 March 1968, p. 11.

14. Brendon, P. *Books & Bookmen,* July 1968, p. 32.

15. Brickhouse, Bob. "Styron Studied the 'Human Terms' of Slavery," *Richmond Times Dispatch,* 15 April 1971, p. 1.

16. Bronner, F.L. "The Historian and William Styron." *New York State Education,* 55 (January 1968), 34.

17. Brown, C.M. *Negro Digest,* 17 (February 1968), 51.

18. Bryden, R. *New Statesman,* 3 May 1968, p. 586.

19. Buckmaster, H. *Christian Science Monitor,* 12 October 1967, p. 11.

20. Bunke, Joan. "Styron Novel is Powerful as Fiction and Sermon," *Des Moines (Iowa) Register*, 15 October 1967, Sec. T, p. 7.

21. Callanan, Kathleen B. "Curl Up and Read," *Seventeen* (January 1968), 116.

22. Charles, R.J. *Book World*, 31 March 1968, p. 11.

23. *Choice*, March 1968, p. 54.

24. Clemons, Joel. "Author Dramatizes Event Masterfully," *Charleston News Courier*, 31 December 1967, Sec. D., p. 2.

25. Coles, R. *Partisan Review*, 35 (Winter 1968), 128.

26. Collier, Peter. "Saga of Rebellion," *The Progressive* (December 1967), 41-42.

27. *"Confessions of Nat Turner* Condemned as Racist Book," *Los Angeles Free Press*, 29 March 1968, p. 8.

28. Cook, B. *National Observer*, 9 October 1967, p. 22.

29. Cooke, M. *Yale Review*, 57 (Winter 1968), 273.

30. Cunningham, Dick. "Styron Writes of Negro with Inside-Out View," *Minneapolis Tribune*, 8 October 1967, Sec. E, p. 6.

31. Currie, Edward. "Author William Styron—Era's Clarion," *Rocky Mountain News* (Denver), 22 October 1967, Startime Section, p. 19.

32. Delany, Lloyd Tom. "A Psychologist Looks at *The Confessions of Nat Turner*," *Psychology Today*, 1 (January 1968), 11-14.

33. Driver, Tom F. "Black Consciousness Through a White Scrim," *Motive*, 27 (February 1968), 56-58.

34. Duberman, Martin. *Village Voice*, 14 December 1967, pp. 8-9, 16.

35. Duffer, Ken. "Nat Turner: Slave to a Terrible Vision," *Winston-Salem (N.C.) Journal and Sentinel,* 8 October 1967, Sec. D, p. 6.

36. E.P.H. *Saturday Review of Literature,* 15 September 1951, p. 12.

37. Enright, D.J. *Listener,* 2 May 1968, p. 558.

38. Fadiman, Clifton. *Book-of-the-Month-Club News,* October 1967, pp. 2-5.

39. Fauchereau, Serge. "Uncle Nat et Oncle Tom," *Quinzaine Litteraire,* 1 April 1969, pp. 5-6.

40. Ferguson, Charles A. "Styron Revises Story of Slave Revolt of 1831," *New Orleans Times Picayune,* 29 October 1967, p. 12.

41. Fremont-Smith, Eliot. "A Sword Is Sharpened." *New York Times,* 3 October 1967, p. 45.

42. Fremont-Smith, Eliot. " 'The Confessions of Nat Turner'—II." *New York Times,* 4 October 1967, p. 45.

43. Fremont-Smith, Eliot. "Nat Turner I: The Controversy." *New York Times,* 1 August 1968, p. 29.

44. Fremont-Smith, Eliot. "Nat Turner II: What Myth Will Serve?" *New York Times,* 2 August 1968, p. 31.

45. Fuller, E. *Wall Street Journal,* 4 October 1967, p. 16.

46. Geismar, Maxwell. "Domestic Tragedy in Virginia," *Saturday Review,* 15 September 1951, pp. 12-13.

47. Gilman, Richard. *New Republic,* 27 April 1968, pp. 23-32.

48. Goodheart, Eugene. "When Slaves Revolt," *Midstream,* 14 (January 1968), 69-72.

49. Greenwood, Walter B. "Nat Turner's Revolt a Tragic Comment on Slavery's Evils," *Buffalo (N.Y.) Evening News,*

14 October 1967, Sec. B., p. 12.

50. Grennan, J. *American Scholar*, 37 (Summer 1968), 528.

51. Griffin, L.W. *Library Journal*, 1 October 1967, p. 3448.

52. Grimes, Roy. "Books and Things—*The Confessions of Nat Turner*," *Victoria (B.C.) Advocate*, 15 October 1967, p. 10.

53. H., S. "Novel of Slave Revolt Eloquent," *San Antonio Express*, 8 October 1967, Sec. II, p. 3.

54. Hall, Joan Joffe. "Jehovah's Rebel Slave," *Houston Post*, 27 October 1967, Spotlight Section, p. 12.

55. Hallie, P.P. *American Scholar*, 37 (Summer 1968), p. 530.

56. Hamilton, Charles V. *Saturday Review*, 22 June 1968, pp. 22-23.

57. Harnack, Curtis. *Kenyon Review*, 30, i (1968), 125.

58. Hassan, Ihab. "The Avant Garde: Which Way Is Forward?" *Nation*, 18 November 1961, pp. 396-399.

59. Heise, Kenan. *Extension*, 62 (December 1967), 54.

60. Herman, Dick. "Is Grim Message of Slavery Just Beginning to be Felt?" *Lincoln (Neb.) Journal and Star*, 15 October 1967, Sec. F, p. 15.

61. Hicks, Granville, *Saturday Review*, 7 October 1967, pp. 29-30.

62. Hicks, Granville. *Saturday Review*, 30 December 1967, p. 19.

63. Hicks, Walter J. "The Futile Insurrection," *Baltimore Sunday Sun*, 15 October 1967, Sec. D, p. 5.

64. Hogan, William. "William Styron's American Tragedy," *San Francisco Chronicle*, 10 October 1967, p. 39.

66. Hurt, Richard L. "Slavery's Quiet Resistance," *Boston Globe*, 8 October 1967, Sec. A., p. 43.

67. Ingle, H.L. "Meditation on History," *Chattanooga (Tenn.) Times*, 12 November 1967, p. 30.

68. Kauffmann, Stanley. *Hudson Review*, 20 (Winter 1967-68), 675.

69. Kazin, Alfred. *Book World*, 8 October 1967, pp. 1, 22.

70. Kincaid, A. *Library Journal*, 15 November 1967, p. 4274.

71. King, L. *America*, 24 February 1968, p. 269.

72. *Kirkus*, 1 August 1967, p. 905.

73. Kirsch, Robert R. "The Virginia Slave Revolt," *Los Angeles Times*, 8 October 1967, p. 36.

74. Krupat, A. *Catholic World*, 206 (February 1968), 226.

75. LaHaye, J. *Best Sellers*, 1 November 1967, p. 308.

76. Layton, Mike. "A Negro Slave Revolt and What It Tells Us," *Olympia (Wash.) Sunday Olympian*, 28 October 1967, p. 27.

77. Lehan, Richard. *Contemporary Literature*, 9 (Autumn 1968), 540-542.

78. Lewis, Claude. "Slavery, Murder, and God," *Philadelphia Sunday Bulletin*, 15 October 1967, Books and Art Section, p. 3.

79. Long, James, *Oregon Journal* (Portland), 11 November 1967, Sec. J, p. 6.

80. McCormick, Jay. "An American Tragedy—Lessons That The Gallows Failed to Teach," *Detroit News*, 8 October 1967, Sec. E, p. 3.

81. McGroaty, Rev. Joseph G. "Nat Turner: A Racial Tract For Our Times," *The Tablet*, 60 (November 16, 1967), 13.

82. McNeill, Robert. *Presbyterian Survey,* 58 (February 1968), 26-27.

83. McPherson, J.L. *Dissent,* 15 (January-February 1968), 86.

84. Malin, Irving. "Nat's Confessions," *University of Denver Quarterly,* 3 (Winter 1968), 94-96.

85. Malone, D. *American Scholar,* 38 (Summer 1968), 532.

86. Mason, Robert. "A Brilliant 'Meditation on History'—Nat Turner, From Birth to Rebellion," *Virginian Pilot and Postsmouth Star,* 8 October 1967, Sec. C, p. 6.

87. Mayes, H.R. *Saturday Review,* 7 October 1967, p. 14.

88. Meras, Phyllis. "Phyllis Meras interviews William Styron," *Saturday Review,* 7 October 1967, p. 30.

89. Meyer, June. "Spokesmen for the Blacks," *The Nation,* 205 (December 4, 1967), 597.

90. Miller, William L. *Reporter,* 16 November 1967, pp. 42-46.

91. Monaghan, Charles. "Portrait of a Man Reading," *Book World,* 27 October 1968, p. 8.

92. Moody, Minnie Hite. "Documentary Novel is Pegged to 1831 Revolt," *Columbus (Ohio) Dispatch,* 22 October 1967, TAB Section, p. 14.

93. Moynahan, J. *Observer,* 5 May 1968, p. 652.

94. Murray, A. *New Leader,* 4 December 1967, p. 18.

95. "Nat Turner's No Longer Unknown—1831 Insurrection Gets a Timely Revival in 'Confession,' " *Grand Rapids (Mich.) Press,* 8 October 1967, p. 39.

96. Newcomb, Horace. "William Styron and the Act of Memory: *The Confessions of Nat Turner,*" *Chicago Review,* 20, i (1968), 86-94.

97. Nolte, William H. "Fact Novel of Revolt in Hot Summer of 1831," *St. Louis Sunday Post-Dispatch*, 8 October 1967, Sec. D., p. 4.

98. O'Connell, Shaun. *The Nation*, 16 October 1967, pp. 373-374.

99. Parker, Roy, Jr. "Styron's 'Nat Turner'—Fact Transmuted into Art," *Raleigh (N.C.) News and Observer*, 30 October 1967, Sec. III, p. 3.

100. Penne, Leo. "Out From the Vicious Circle," *Seattle Post-Intelligencer*, 22 October 1967, Northwest Today Section, p. 4.

101. Petersen, C. *Book World*, 29 September 1968, p. 21.

102. Plimpton, George. "William Styron: A Shared Ordeal," *New York Times Book Review*, 8 October 1967, pp. 2, 3, 30, 32, 34.

103. Prescott, Orville. "Books of the Times," *New York Times*, 10 September 1951, p. 19.

104. Price, R.G. *Punch*, 1 May 1968, p. 652.

105. *Publisher's Weekly*, 31 July 1967, p. 53.

106. Q., G. "Revolt of Negro Slaves Echoes Over the Years," *Waco (Texas) Tribune-Herald*, 5 November 1967, Sec. D, p. 13.

107. Quarles, B. *Social Studies*, 59 (November 1968), 280.

108. Rahv, Philip. "Through the Midst of Jerusalem," *New York Review of Books*, 26 October 1967, pp. 6-10.

109. Redding, Saunders. *American Scholar*, 37 (Summer 1968), 542.

110. Richardson, D.E. "Telling All?" *Shenandoah*, 19 (Autumn 1967), 84-87.

111. Richter, David H. *Chicago Literary Review*, (October 1967), 1, 10-11.

112. Robertson, Don. "One View: Styron Is a Brave Failure," *Cleveland Plain Dealer*, 15 October 1967, Sec. H, p. 8.

113. Rubin, Louis D., Jr. "Books—Eloquent Story of a Slave Rebellion," *Washington (D.C.) Sunday Star*, 8 October 1967, Sec. G, p. 14.

114. Rubin, Louis D., Jr. "William Styron and Human Bondage: *The Confessions of Nat Turner*," *Hollins Critic*, 14 (December 1967), 1-12.

115. Schaap, Dick. "Framework for Confessions," *San Francisco Sunday Examiner and Chronicle*, 15 October 1967, This World Section, pp. 39, 46.

116. Schlueter, P. *Christian Century*, 21 February 1968, pp. 234-235.

117. Schroth, R.A. *America*, 14 October 1967, p. 416.

118. Schwartz, Joseph. "Negro Revolt of 1831 Flares Again in a 'Big' Novel of Fall," *Milwaukee Journal*, 8 October 1967, Sec. V, p. 4.

119. Shaw, Russell. *The Sign*, 47 (January 1968), 63.

120. Sheed, Wilfrid. "The Slave Who Became a Man," *New York Times*, 8 October 1967, pp. 1-3.

121. Sherman, John K. "Portrays Negro View—Novel Illuminates History of Slavery," *Minneapolis Star*, 10 October 1967, Sec. E, p. 4.

122. Smith, Miles A. "Slave Revolt of 1831 is Recounted," *Indianapolis News*, 21 October 1967, p. 30. See also *St. Louis Globe Democrat*, 21 October 1967, Sec. F, p. 5.

123. Sokolov, Raymond. "Into the Mind of Nat Turner," *Newsweek*, 16 October 1967, pp. 65-69.

124. Steiner, George. "The Fire Last Time," *New Yorker*, 25 November 1967, pp. 236-44.

125. Stevenson, David L. "Fiction's Unfamiliar Face," *The Nation*, 1 November 1958, p. 307.

126. Thomas, Sidney. "Slave Broke His Chains," *Atlanta Journal and Constitution*, 12 November 1967, Sec. D, p. 10.

127. Thompson, John. "Rise and Slay," *Commentary*, 44, v (1967), 81-85.

128. *Time*, 13 October 1967, p. 110.

129. *Times Literary Supplement*, 9 May 1968, p. 480.

130. *Top News*, 24 April 1968, p. 327.

131. Tucker, Martin. *Commonweal*, 22 December 1967, p. 388.

132. Turner, Darwin T. *Journal of Negro History*, 53 (April 1968), 183-186.

133. Turney, Charles. "Virginian's Novel Seeks 'Meditation on History,' " *Richmond (Va.) Times-Dispatch*, 15 October 1967, Sec. F, p. 5.

134. *Virginia Quarterly Review*, 44 (Winter 1968), 8.

135. W., B. "The Negro Fury: A Vital Insight," *Long Beach (Cal.) Independent Press-Telegram*, 18 November 1967, Sec. A, p. 6.

136. Wade, Gerald. "The Only Effective U.S. Negro Revolt," *Omaha (Neb.) World-Herald*, 29 October 1967, Sec, I, p. 36.

137. Waldmeir, Joseph. "Quest Without Faith," *The Nation*, 18 November 1961, pp. 390-96.

138. Walker, A. *American Scholar*, 37 (Summer 1968), 550.

139. Weber, R.B. "Styron's Power Creates a Real Being," *Louisville (Ky.) Times*, 13 October 1967, Sec. A, p. 11.

140. Weeks, Edward. *Atlantic*, November 1967, p. 130.

141. Winfrey, Lee. "When a Negro Slave Rebelled," *Detroit Free Press*, 8 October 1967, Sec. B, p. 5.

142. Wolff, Geoffrey A. "Slavery Intersects Present," *Washington (D.C.) Post*, 24 October 1967, Sec. A, p. 16.

143. Woodward, C. Vann. *New Republic*, 7 October 1967, pp. 25-28.

144. Wright, Giles E. "Life of Real Slave Treated in Top Novel," *Los Angeles Herald Examiner*, 8 October 1967, Sec. J, p. 4.

145. Yardley, Jonathan. "Mr. Styron's Monumental 'Meditation on History,' " *Greensboro (N.C.) Daily News*, 8 October 1967, Sec. D, p. 3.

IN THE CLAP SHACK

1. Barnes, Clive. *New York Times Book Review*, 17 December 1972, p. 1.

2. *Choice*, November 1973, p. 1391.

3. *Book World (Washington Post)*, 15 July 1973, p. 15.

4. Leon, Philip W. *Nashville Tennessean*, 2 September 1973, p. 10-E.

5. *Library Journal*, 1 May 1973, p. 1515.

6. *Library Journal*, 15 October 1973, p. 3018.

7. Malin, Irving. *Southern Literary Journal*, 6 (Spring 1974), 151-157.

8. *Publisher's Weekly*, 7 May 1973, p. 63.

NON-LITERARY REFERENCES TO STYRON IN
THE NEW YORK TIMES

Styron does not shrink from controversy. A solid liberal, he confronts such issues as the 1968 Chicago Democratic Convention, environmental concerns, Nazi concentration camps, Soviet oppression of dissident artists, and civil rights.

1966

1. January 26, p. 14, col. 4

Styron and eight others are named to the National Institute of Arts and Letters.

1967

2. October 19, p. 58, col. 1

Wolper Pictures pay over $600,000 for screen rights to *The Confessions of Nat Turner.*

1968

3. May 7, p. 1, col. 3

Styron wins Pulitzer Prize for fiction. A biographical sketch and picture appear on May 7, p. 34, col. 1. See also May 7, p. 46, col. 1.

4. August 14, p. 40, col. 3

Picture and article on Styron. Styron is co-chairman, with George Plimpton, of a fund raising party to aid Senator Eugene J. Mc-Carthy in his presidential campaign.

1969

5.   August 12, p. 36, col. 7

Styron expresses fears that Anatoly Kuznet-sov's defection may endanger Soviet dissenters still in the USSR. The 39-year old Soviet author received asylum in Britain, 30 July 1969.

6.   August 27, p. 42, col. 5

A letter by J.R. Davis calls Styron's charac-terization of Kuznetsov's defection as "betrayal" a measure of the agonizing dilemma of Soviet writers.

7.   September 4, p. 46, col. 4

L. Krzyzanowski replies to the letter of J.R. Davis of August 27.

8.   September 14, Sect. IV, p. 13, col. 1

Styron clarifies his criticism of Kuznetsov's defection by saying he questions Kuznetsov's "precipitate haste" in implicating other Soviet writers in a way which may threaten their security.

9.   March 31, p. 28, col. 1

David L. Wolper yields to pressure from the Black Anti-Defamation Association and agrees not to use "The Confessions of Nat Turner" as the title for the movie version of Styron's book; he also agrees to use several other his-torical sources for the movie. Styron reportedly has no objections.

10.   April 3, p. 42, col. 3

Tom Wicker criticizes the changes in the film about Nat Turner which were made to meet black objections.

11.   December 13, p. 19, col. 3

Styron testifies that he saw police beat demon
strators in Lincoln Park in Chicago on August
24 during the Democratic National Convention
He said he saw police push demonstrators
through the glass windows of the Haymarket
Lounge.

1970

12.   January 28, p. 48, col. 1

Styron charges that the filming of *The Confessions of Nat Turner*, which has been temporari-
ly postponed, is being influenced by "black
pressure groups" who oppose his treatment
of Turner; he says the film studio, 20th Century
Fox, is being intimidated into changing the
film version in order to placate both black mili-
tants and whites.

13.   February 23, p. 24, col. 2

English teacher Mrs. C. Hanover, Roxbury,
Connecticut, is suspended for refusing to say
the Pledge of Allegiance with her classes; her
lawyers have obtained a court order requiring
the school system to show cause why she should
not be reinstated. A hearing is planned for Su-
perior Court. Over two dozen local residents,
including Styron and Arthur Miller, sign a
statement protesting the suspension.

14.   March 14, p. 28, col. 4 and May 27, p. 40, col. 1

Styron wins the Howells Medal of the American Academy of Arts and Letters.

1971

15.   March 10, p. 40, col. 7

Styron, Bernard Malamud, and John Updike
have been appointed honorary consultants
in American letters at the Library of Congress
for the next three years. They will advise on

acquisitions of literary works and will recommend projects.

16.   August 12, p. 17, col. 5

The National Conference on Soviet Jewry will issue a booklet containing English translations of works by several Soviet poets. In a separate appeal, one hundred writers and scholars write to Soviet President Podgorny urging him to restore to Soviet Jews their fundamental human right to create cultural and educational facilities. Among the signers of the appeal are Styron, Saul Bellow, Herbert Mitgang, Malcolm Cowley, Bernard Malamud, Louis Auchincloss, Norman Mailer, Lionel Trilling, and Rex Stout.

1973

17.   November 10, p. 37, col. 4

Styron confirms that he and three partners, writer Philip Roth, director Mike Nichols, and producer L. Allen, have bought a two hundred-plus acre tract of land near Kent, Connecticut, for "several hundred thousand dollars." He says their main interest is in keeping the land as open space.

1974

18.   June 25, p. 27, col. 1

Styron reflects on his recent visit to the remains of Auschwitz concentration camp; he calls the holocaust so "awesomely central to our present-day consciousness" that one shrinks from the knowledge that one million Christians also died with six million Jews. Styron calls Nazi totalitarianism anti-Christian as well as anti-Semitic. Illustrations on page 37, col. 3.

19.   July 24, p. 40, col. 4

A letter from James Parks Morton, Edith Wyshogrod, Rosemary Ruether, Michael D. Ryan and Irving Greenberg on Styron's June 25 article on the Auschwitz conference held at Cathedral Church of St. John the Divine, New York City, says the silence of institutional Christianity during the Nazi period remains a fact to be dealt with.

1977

20.   May 16, p. 33, col. 1

Styron delivers an eulogy, along with Willie Morris and Irwin Shaw, for James Jones at a memorial service at Bridgehampton Community House; 400 people attend the service.

INDEX OF NAMES

SUBJECT INDEX

ABOUT THE COMPILER

Philip W. Leon is assistant professor of English at
The Citadel, Charleston, South Carolina. He has
had articles published in *Southern Literary Journal*
and *Notes on Teaching English*.